A Heart that Worships

A Heart that Worships

YOUR SECRET WEAPON OF POWER AND VICTORY

Tamara Hardy

Pour Out Your Spirit Publishing, LLC
Richmond, Virginia

Copyright © 2021 by Tamara D. Hardy

All rights reserved. No part of this book may be reproduced or used in any manner without the written permission of the copyright owner except for the use of quotations in a book review.

FIRST EDITION

The following abbreviations are used to identify versions of the Bible used in this book.

KJV *King James Version*, also known as the *Authorized Version*. (Public Domain).

NKJV Scripture is taken from the New King James Version®. Copyright © 1982 by Thomas Nelson. Used by permission. All rights reserved.

NLT Scripture quotations are taken from the Holy Bible, New Living Translation, copyright ©1996, 2004, 2007, 2013, 2015 by Tyndale House Foundation. Used by permission of Tyndale House Publishers, Inc., Carol Stream, Illinois 60188. All rights reserved.

NIV Scripture quotations marked (NIV) are taken from the Holy Bible, New International Version®, NIV®. Copyright © 1973, 1978, 1984, 2011 by Biblica, Inc.™ Used by permission of Zondervan. All rights reserved worldwide. www.zondervan.com. The "NIV" and "New International Version" are trademarks registered in the United States Patent and Trademark Office by Biblica, Inc.™

AMP Scripture quotations marked (AMP) are taken from the Amplified Bible, Copyright © 2015 by The Lockman Foundation. Used by permission.

ESV The ESV® Bible (The Holy Bible, English Standard Version®) copyright © 2001 by Crossway Bibles, a publishing ministry of Good News Publishers. ESV Text Edition: 2016. The ESV® text has been reproduced in cooperation with and by permission of Good News Publishers. Unauthorized reproduction of this publication is prohibited. All rights reserved.

CEV   Scripture is taken from the Contemporary English Version © 1991, 1992, 1995 by American Bible Society, Used by Permission.

Because of the dynamic nature of the Internet, any web addresses or links contained in this book may have changed since publication and may no longer be valid.

The book cover image is stock imagery used by permission from Pixels.com.

Nouns and pronouns referring to deity are capitalized throughout the text of this book unless they are included within a direct quotation, in which case the original capitalization is retained.

For literary emphasis, all references to the noun **satan** throughout the book are in lowercase.

Illustrations by Michael E. Hardy

Cover design by Michaela F. Hardy

Printed in the United States of America, December 2020

ISBN-13: 9781735903033

Pour Out Your Spirit Publishing, LLC

www.poyspublishing.com

www.poyspublishing@gmail.com

Contents

ix

Dedication *xi*

Acknowledgements *xiii*

1. Introduction *1*
2. Are You Ashamed To Worship God? *7*
3. Nine Steps to a Heart that Worships *15*
4. A Heart That Knows It Is Not Improper or Out of Control to Freely Worship *19*
5. A Heart Willing to Repent *31*
6. A Heart Yielded to the Holy Spirit *39*
7. A Heart that Understands the Role of the Holy Spirit in a Christian's life *53*
8. A Heart Free of Condemnation for Past Sins *69*
9. A Heart Wanting More Than a Casual Relationship with God *75*
10. A Heart that Chooses Christ Instead of Religion *81*
11. A Heart Healed of Wounds from the Past *91*
12. A Heart that Accepts Jesus' Sacrifice on the Cross for Our Sins *99*
13. Eight Important Reasons to Worship *105*

14. Worship is An Act of Love Between You and God
111

15. Worship is a Form of WARFARE Against the Kingdom of Darkness
119

125

16. Worship Allows Us to Receive the Ability of God   *139*

17. Worship Imparts to Us the Mind of God   *145*

18. Worship Bestows Upon Us the Anointing of God with Power
151

19. Worship Enables You to Overcome Grief and Sorrow
159

20. Worship Breaks the Power of Demonic Bondage   *169*

21. Worship illuminates the Soul with the Light of the Holy Spirit and the Word of God
177

Bibliography   *187*

Dedication

IN MEMORY OF ERIC DARRYL WILLIAMS (BROTHER)

JANUARY 4, 1962 – MAY 6, 2018

AND

ELLA GILES HARDY (MOTHER IN LAW)

OCTOBER 23, 1938 – JUNE 25, 2020

FOREVER IN OUR HEARTS

Acknowledgements

Thank you, Jesus! You are the author, and finisher of my faith. You put a smile on my face when I think of you and call your name. I enjoy our fellowship together and I am so grateful for your passion to fulfill the Fathers' will!

Father, I thank you for my husband, Pastor Michael Hardy, who was so excited and amazed that I was writing a book that you wanted to tell the world despite my protests. I also want to thank my husband, that over thirty-eight years ago, you chose to make Jesus, not only Savior but Lord of your life. That day changed our marriage and our future. Thank you for being a loving Father to our two children and for working so hard over the years to provide for our family.

To my adult children, Jordan Elisha and Michaela Faith, when I think of you I have so many emotions that I find it hard to express them. I thank God for sending you to your Father and me. You have blessed us more than you will ever know. It has truly, truly been a joy raising you, not because your Father and I were perfect nor were you perfect. The Lord gave us all balance. He smoothed the crooked places and He repaired the breaches along the way in our relationships, attitudes, and direction. I am so proud of you both and who you have become. I also love how you treat one another with love and respect. All the glory belongs to Jesus for it all!

I am forever grateful to the following people who contributed their time and talents to help me complete this book: Michael Hardy, Jordan Hardy, Michaela Hardy, Debbie Cohen, Cynthia Ellenwood, Dianna Jones. Thank you to my pastors, Bishop Marvin Mason and Pastor Kate Mason for your leadership, support, and input.

To the Manna Christian Fellowship Church family, I wish I could thank you one by one for your ministry to Christ that has impacted my life. I especially want to thank the intercessory prayer, missions, and the praise and worship ministries I have been privileged to serve with.

Finally to Bishop Wellington Boone, thank you for your encouragement to me and so many others to be a witness of Jesus Christ in lifestyle and the written word.

1

Introduction

This book is written for the hungry heart who is searching for the meaning of true worship and how to move into deeper realms of worship and intimacy with God.

This book will help you examine your heart, your mind, and your beliefs and discover what could be a stumbling block keeping you from the best life God has to offer you. The best God has to give you is Himself! When you have God, you truly have everything you will ever need. You will learn more about this truth as you read about the nine steps you should follow to develop a heart that worships. A heart that worships is a heart that dwells in the presence of God.

Finally, you will learn about the rewards or benefits of worshiping God which is life-changing.

If you discover any areas in your life that you need to repent for or ask healing for as you read, don't hesitate to do so right away. Don't delay!

We were created to worship God, and our soul longs for a relationship with Him.

The contents of this book are based on the Holy Bible which unfolds and reveals God and His "triune" nature. He is God the Father, God the Son, and God the Holy Spirit. Each of the three is God, yet separate; together all three reflect the complete nature and personality of God. Each will be spoken of throughout this book.

There is a hunger within everyone born to know God our Creator. As we journey through life, we want to know why we were born. Why are we here? What is life all about? What is our purpose for living? All the answers to these questions and more are found in knowing God.

> "My soul (my life, my inner self) longs for and greatly desires the courts of the Lord; My heart and my flesh sing for joy to the living God" (Psalm 84:2 AMP).

We were created to worship God, and our soul longs for a relationship with Him. Until we discover that truth, there will always be something missing in our lives. In my experience, people try to fill the void in their life through money, work, relationships, fame, or fortune. However, nothing will be able to satisfy and fulfill that longing but God. That is because you are so much more than your physical body and your personality (soul). You also possess a spirit just as God, your creator, is a spirit. Your spirit was created so that God could dwell in you!

Your life is about to change marvelously because you are seeking greater truth and a deeper understanding of what it means to be a worshiper. It is a noble and worthwhile pursuit to know God in His completeness.

> *"You will seek me and find me when you seek me with all your heart"* (Jeremiah 29:13 NIV).

Truly the Lord will fulfill His promise in this scripture. *You will find Him* when you seek Him with all your heart. Seek Him with everything you have. Desire His word in the Holy Bible the way you desire daily food. Pray without ceasing and seek to know His will about everything. Do what He directs you to do in His word and in prayer. Give Him your whole heart. Not just a part but, all of your heart. That's what a worshiper does. A worshiper's heart belongs to God.

When your heart belongs to God then you will want to tell Him how much you appreciate His love, His blessings, His mercy, and His grace that you see at work daily in your life.

The more important your relationship with God becomes, the more you will want to be around Him and enjoy His presence and sweet fellowship. Yes, that is possible! You can fellowship with God the Father, Jesus, and the Holy Spirit! If you have accepted Jesus Christ as your personal Savior then you have been born into your spiritual family. You now have a heavenly Father. His first-born son is Jesus and you are now another one of His children. The Holy Spirit is also a part of the family and He wants to be your constant companion, helper, mentor, and friend.

God wants to draw closer to you than you do to Him! He created us as sons and daughters to love and to fellowship with. Our worship rendered to God is our expression of love toward Him. Our worship is reverence or respect for the Most Holy God, who also happens to be our daddy (Abba which means father). Our worship is our gratefulness to Jesus for His sacrifice on the cross to save us from our sins. Our worship is our fellowship with the Holy Spirit who is leading and guiding us into all truth. Hallelujah for the Godhead three in one!

God wants to draw closer to you than you do to Him!

When we enter true worship, God is present. If God is present, then everything we need is present! However, we don't worship God to get our needs met. It's just an added benefit of His presence. He deserves the glory and praise regardless of what He's done for us, but just for who He is.

> *"You will show me the way of life, granting me the joy your presence and the pleasures of living with you forever"* (Psalm 16:11 NLT).

There is an abundant life waiting for you in the bosom of the Father at the leading of the Holy Spirit and in the Lordship of our Savior Jesus Christ. It's yours but, you must want it as if it were a precious gem and a hidden treasure of great value that money could never buy. Just to be in the presence of the Creator of the universe; the almighty God is incredible. To know that one so powerful could also be your heavenly Father is amazing. Yet in His role as your Father, He wants to lovingly lead you, teach you, fellowship with you and bless you. He alone wants to be the object of your worship.

So many believers have accepted Jesus Christ as their personal Savior but, they don't desire to spend any personal time with Him. They don't see the need to. Jesus, God the Father, and the Holy Spirit are not real persons to them.

However, that is not the truth. They are more real than your natural father, mother, sister, and brother. You and I would not be here on the earth if it were not for them.

I hope you will awaken to the reality that everything around you worships God; the trees, mountains, seas, rocks, every flying creature, and every living thing. Every living thing was created for His purposes but, you, however, were created in His likeness and image to become a part of His family. Don't take that for granted. Don't dismiss it. Receive the wonderful invitation from the Most High God to become one of His sons or daughters. Let Him be your Father who will love, protect, and guide you all of your days. No matter what challenges lie ahead, you can weather every storm knowing that His presence is with you and inside of you.

May you live a life, from this moment forth, where you dwell in the presence of the Lord. May He grant you the joy of His presence and His pleasures forevermore.

2

Are You Ashamed To Worship God?

I can recall a time in the past, during a Sunday morning service, when the Spirit of God was so intense and so sweet as the congregation sang together. Such sweet harmonies were being sung by many in the congregation. They began to "speak in tongues" which means to speak in a heavenly language or tongue that is unknown or unfamiliar to the person speaking. If you are unfamiliar with this terminology or action, it is described in the Bible in Acts 2:4. This scripture and book of the Bible describe the first account of the church receiving this "gift of tongues" when the Holy Spirit came into the earth to begin His ministry as He still does today.

On that Sunday morning as the congregation sang and worshipped, I witnessed some members even singing a heavenly song in the Spirit. That means they sang a new song they had never heard nor sung before that was given to them by the same Holy Spirit. If you can imagine the sound of a congregation singing in an unknown language, in beautiful harmony worshiping the Lord – it was amazing and so anointed. I felt such peace and such love; I felt complete in God.

As I listened to the sound of worship, I wanted to raise my hands so desperately and join in and simply surrender but, I did not dare! My eyes were closed and so, I said this to the Lord within my thoughts, "Lord, my hands may not be lifted on the outside but, they are lifted on the inside." Even though I knew we were in the midst of a visitation from the Lord, I was ashamed to lift my hands and open my mouth to worship the King of Kings and the Lord of Lords. I was "embarrassed" to demonstrate worship in that way publicly. You see, I held in higher regard the opinions of the people around me and what they thought of me rather than what I thought about Jesus who saved me, washed me, and gave me eternal life. My pride was more important to me than embracing the presence of the Holy One.

The amazing thing is, I am sure that no one was even paying any attention to me! It was a figment of my imagination. They were focused on Jesus just as I should have been.

What held me back from lifting my hands openly or rendering any type of expression as a sign of my joy and gratitude to the Lord? It was my carnal nature that had not yet been put under the control of my spirit. In other words, my pride was stronger than my spirit, which understood that

God was near and longed for me to worship Him without limitations. My outward actions followed the inward desires of my heart. I desired to be accepted by men and women more than I desired to please God so, I acted accordingly.

Did that mean that I wasn't a born-again believer? Not at all. I was still a believer. I just needed to take a step of faith, by my will, and do what my flesh did not want to do, which was to worship the Lord. Our flesh never wants to do what is good or just. By nature, our flesh is carnal and self-serving. I needed to allow my spirit, which was leading me to worship, to reign over my carnal nature which didn't want to.

It is interesting how we can be so devoted to our favorite sports team and eagerly associate ourselves with their victories and their defeats. We have no problem reacting emotionally to what is happening during the course of a game or a season. If our team is losing, it may actually affect our emotions and attitudes. For some, it has a greater effect than others. If our team is winning then we gladly express it with smiles, laughter, happiness, or even bragging. It's so easy to understand what being a "fan (fanatic)" is all about in the sports world. We are not shocked at seeing sports arenas filled with screaming, jeering fans some of whom actually worship their team or specific players. They have studied the stats of their team thoroughly. They know the players, coaches, and they can discuss in detail the plays and other particulars. They own team memorabilia and they may even follow the personal lives of the team players. Their devotion to the game and their team is unsurpassed. They are completely devoted to their team and don't you ever bad-mouth them! They have no problem freely expressing their devotion publicly at games or at home in front of the TV, or in conversations with others.

How is it that sports fans can out praise and out worship most Christian believers? Why are so many of us ashamed of being a "fan (fanatic)" for Christ?

> **Praise and worship are the "atmosphere" in all of heaven.**

When I think about heaven, I don't believe it is a quiet place, as many of our churches are. In fact, the Bible gives clear images of heaven as a busy place of activity, the least of which is continual praise and worship of God. There are four and twenty elders who bow down before the throne of God and cast their crowns! I imagine that must make some noise, right? I am certain that great exuberance and praise are going on continually in every part of heaven. Praise and worship are the "atmosphere" in all of heaven. It is all around in what you smell, feel, breathe, and think. All those who are there, are in God's house. They are not guests once they arrive. Heaven becomes their home too! They belong there with the light of the world, the lily of the valley, the bright and morning star whose name is Jesus.

When you have developed a relationship with God, and you have a revelation of who God is and what He sacrificed just to get to you and rescue you, then you really can't keep silent in His presence. When you understand how much He risked coming to the earth to be crucified to bring you back to the Father, it won't matter what anyone thinks about your praise, worship, and adoration. You will not care about them because He cared so much about you! You will not be ashamed to worship openly before men, women, boys, and girls. Like the sports fanatic, you are devoted to your master, Savior, and Lord, and you are not concerned about what anyone thinks about it.

Your freedom to sing, shout, dance, and lift your hands comes when Christ has been revealed to you by the Holy Spirit. You must be careful not to stagnate or stop growing after you have been converted. Just as a baby eventually learns to take His first steps, you must grow beyond your initial salvation experience and learn to walk by the Spirit. Your Spirit will only grow because you feed it Spiritual food so, you must feed it the Word of God. You must nourish it with prayer and thanksgiving. You must nurture it with a lifestyle of praise and worship.

Praise can take many forms throughout your day. You may be on your job concentrating on your tasks at hand and you begin to think about the Lord. You can take the time to tell Him in your thoughts words, such as "I love you Lord", then get back to work. Throughout the day, you can have moments or minutes where you sing in your Spirit a worship song that you love so much or that you heard at church last week. You may want to pray for a few seconds in your thoughts because you need help with your job, or a co-worker needs your prayer. Of course, you can simply set aside devotion time in the morning, lunchtime, or in the evening. All of these suggestions are ways that you help your Spirit grow and find that Christ is revealed more and more to you.

There should come a time when you never go through a day not thinking about Him, thanking Him, praising Him, blessing Him, praying for His guidance, repenting to Him, and talking to Him about anything and everything. As you do this on a daily basis, your life will be hidden in Christ and His in yours! You will feel the Holy Spirit on the inside of you instantly when you just turn your attention to Him. You will love being in His presence at any time and at any place. He will literally help you and advise you in every situation – and I do mean anything! Just be prepared for His answers because they are not always yes. His answers may be no also.

Also, you must be prepared to obey Him. His walking, talking, and leading you are entirely dependent upon your obedience to what He tells you to do. The more you seek His guidance and obey Him, the closer you will be drawn to Him. Likewise, the less you seek His guidance and the less you obey Him, the further away from Him you will become. The Holy Spirit never forces Himself on anyone or barges His way into anyone's life. We must want Him in our lives. We must want the Lord's guidance, His wisdom, and His righteousness. We must want Him! When we don't want the Lord to draw near to us, He won't. The Lord will not stay where He's not invited. I'm the same way. Aren't you?

When you decide that you want to continually grow in the Spirit, and you won't shun the spiritual gifts revealed in the Bible as not applicable to you, your hunger will be satisfied by the Holy Spirit. Your hunger for more of God will enable you to understand the Word of God to a greater measure.

The Holy Spirit will reveal to you the Jesus "*since He always lives to make intercession for them*" as Hebrews 7:25 (KJV) states below,

> "*Therefore He is also able to save [a]to the uttermost those who come to God through Him, since He always lives to make intercession for them.*".

Your hunger will permit the Holy Spirit to lead you into all truth. You won't struggle to worship publicly because you will already be worshiping privately. Worship will become your new normal.

Will you become a fanatic for Jesus? I hope you say a resounding "Yes"! Will you care about what others think? I hope the answer will be definitely "No"! I hope you would not dare to trade your life in Christ for anything in this world.

You will not be in this world forever. Your eternal home is in heaven and when you cross over to eternity you will be in good company with the saints and heavenly beings who worship the King of Kings and the Lord of Lords.

3

Nine Steps to a Heart that Worships

In the next several chapters, you are going to discover nine steps to keep your heart open to the word of God, the Holy Spirit, and the will of God for your life. These steps will also teach you how to protect your heart from hurt, fear, pride, and attacks of the enemy satan. This is crucial to living a victorious life and developing a heart that worships. If you have struggled in any of these areas in the past, it may have hindered your ability to worship God as freely and fully as you desire. It may have caused you to have a distorted view of God and His love and determination to give you salvation through His son Jesus Christ.

As you read these chapters, you will not only discover areas we all may struggle with but also how to overcome and move forward in freedom and victory.

I encourage you to take your time and examine each subject and ask the Holy Spirit to reveal to you if any have been or continue to be a challenge for you. Maybe you are thankfully free in those areas but, you have loved ones, friends, or acquaintances whom you know that need this truth to be revealed in their lives. Pass this along and pray for them to receive what the Holy Spirit wants to reveal to them and heal them from all ailments. There's no greater blessing you can give someone than salvation, freedom from bondage, and the right perspective on their destiny in Christ Jesus.

Let's list each of the nine steps to worship below:

1. *A Heart that Knows it is Not Improper or Out of Control to Freely Worship.*
2. *A Heart Willing to Repent.*
3. *A Heart Yielded to the Holy Spirit.*
4. *A Heart that Understands the Role of the Holy Spirit in a Christian's life.*
5. *A Heart Free of Condemnation for Past Sins.*
6. *A Heart Wanting More Than a Casual Relationship with God.*
7. *A Heart that Chooses Christ Instead of Religion.*
8. *A Heart Healed of Wounds from the Past.*
9. *A Heart that Accepts Jesus Sacrifice on the Cross for Our Sins.*

Before we begin to explore each chapter, repeat this simple prayer of faith that this time, will not only be fruitful but, will be life-changing:

> *Heavenly Father, I come to you now in the precious name of Jesus the Messiah. I want to know how to worship you, Lord, in a greater way than I do today. I am seeking a closer relationship with you dear Lord. Please come into my heart and cleanse me from all unrighteousness. I open my heart to the truth you have to share with me. Help me to receive it and to know it is from you. I give you permission to shine your light on any areas you want me to acknowledge and repent of. I give you permission to bring deliverance into my soul. I thank you dear Holy Spirit that you will lead and guide me into all truth as I read this book and as I also read your Word. Thank you, Lord, that I will never be the same. In Jesus' name, I pray. Amen.*

4

A Heart That Knows It Is Not Improper or Out of Control to Freely Worship

Let's take a look at the meaning of the word worship according to Merriam-Webster's collegiate dictionary, from http://www.merriam-webster.com/dictionary/worship):

> **Definition of worship (Entry 2 of 2)**
>
> 1: reverence offered a divine being or supernatural power also: an act of expressing such reverence.
>
> 2: a form of religious practice with its creed and ritual.
>
> 3: extravagant respect or admiration for or devotion to an object of esteem worship of the dollar.

Worship is a demonstration of the reality of the worthiness of God. First, let's look at the meaning of the word demonstrate. To demonstrate is clearly to show the existence or truth of (something) by giving proof or evidence. It means to establish, prove, show, or substantiate something (taken from https://www.learnersdictionary.com/definition/demonstrating). To demonstrate is to point out something. Now let's look again at the word worship. It means worthiness, respect, and honor paid to a divine being. The origin of the word worship is worth-ship, which is the acknowledgment of worth. Worship is an outward demonstration that clearly shows the proof and gives evidence that God the Father, Jesus the Son, and the Holy Spirit are worthy of our respect, reverence, thanksgiving, and honor and all praise! Worship must be demonstrated! It must be an action carried out on our part as believers. Worship is the response of every believer to His or her God. It is a response of love! God expects every born again, washed in the blood believer to worship Him!

Worship is not the responsibility of the Bishop, Rabbi, Priest, Pastor, or clergy alone to carry out in a church service. It is not the responsibility of the choir and musicians to worship God for everyone else. God expects every born again, washed in the blood believer to worship Him! Can anyone else worship God for you? No, they cannot. You are the only one who can thank God for saving your soul and for what he's done in your life. He was the only perfect sacrifice that could die on the cross to save your soul. What He did was for you! *You* are the only one who can receive that personal sacrifice for *your* sins, and *you* are the only one who can thank Him, praise Him, and worship Him for it.

How is it that in some of our local churches, we have come up with programs, formats, and rituals that don't allow very much freedom to worship God? Please understand that this is not a criticism of the need to keep order in the church. Certainly, we need to ensure that nothing takes place that would dishonor God or grieve the Holy Spirit. God is a God of order and we have nothing to fear about being out of order or out of control if we give the Holy Spirit the reins to our service. He is a gentleman and He will keep order. We just don't want to become afraid or opposed to what He would allow to take place that is according to the word of God.

If it is according to the word of God, how is it that we judge it as "out of order". If we are afraid of His spiritual gifts being demonstrated or released in our churches today because the service may get out of control, He won't manifest them. If we believe that the gifts of the Spirit were only for the early church and not today, they won't manifest. The Holy Spirit will continue to minister to us and visit us in our services, as He does today for however long we allow Him to but, He will only do *what* we allow Him to. He will never barge His way into our hearts and lives, and He will never force Himself upon our church. We must put out the welcome mat to Him if we want all that He wants to give us. There is so much He wants to adorn the bride of Christ with!

Many of us have been taught that to be emotional, loud, or "make a scene" in a church service is out of order. The fact is that sometimes what we see demonstrated in the church may be out of order but, not always. Some people believe that an important part of their faith and participation in the congregational worship experience is to demonstrate that they have been "touched" by the Spirit. They may do something physical in the church service, not because they are "moved" by the Holy Spirit but, because they want *others* to see their spirituality. Their focus is on what others will see and believe about them and not what God is genuinely doing inside of them. They may have learned that behavior somewhere in a former or present church. They are in error and they are not responding to the unction (anointing or touch) of the Holy Spirit. They are demonstrating a soulish (not of the spirit) praise and worship of God.

Of course, this causes many others to categorize *anyone* who is genuinely worshiping God under the unction of the Holy Spirit as also out of order in the church because they may be loud or emotional also and their behavior is completely outside of the norm for their church.

How do you tell the difference between the two? As a believer and especially a leader in the church, when you are filled with the Holy Spirit you will know by that same Spirit what is genuine and what is not. Have you heard the phrase, "It takes one to know one?" If you are a worshiper then you can recognize other worshipers. His Spirit inside of you will bear witness of whether His Spirit is operating in another believer. Remember, He wants to keep order in the church too because it is HIS CHURCH!

We need to be able to come to our churches and engage in pure worship. We can't even imagine the power, anointing, healing, deliverance, and most of all, salvation, that would occur whenever believers are freely worshiping together!

> **We need to be able to come to our churches and engage in pure worship.**

You may have heard about the disciples of Jesus in the book of Acts, as they were in the upper room praying together in one accord. There were one hundred and twenty of them together praying and waiting for the Holy Spirit, as Jesus had instructed them before He ascended to heaven. Here is part of that account in the Bible in Acts 2:1-21 (NIV):

> *"When the day of Pentecost came, they were all together in one place. Suddenly a sound like the blowing of a violent wind came from heaven and filled the whole house where they were sitting. They saw what seemed to be tongues of fire that separated and came to rest on each of them. All of them were filled with the Holy Spirit and began to speak in other tongues as the Spirit enabled them. Now there were staying in Jerusalem God-fearing Jews from every nation*

under heaven. When they heard this sound, a crowd came together in bewilderment, because each one heard their own language being spoken. Utterly amazed, they asked: Aren't all these who are speaking Galileans? Then how is it that each of us hears them in our native language? Parthians, Medes and Elamites; residents of Mesopotamia, Judea and Cappadocia, Pontus and Asia, Phrygia and Pamphylia, Egypt and the parts of Libya near Cyrene; visitors from Rome (both Jews and converts to Judaism); Cretans and Arabs—we hear them declaring the wonders of God in our own tongues!" Amazed and perplexed, they asked one another, "What does this mean?" Some, however, made fun of them and said, "They have had too much wine."

Then Peter stood up with the Eleven, raised His voice, and addressed the crowd: "Fellow Jews and all of you who live in Jerusalem, let me explain this to you; listen carefully to what I say. These people are not drunk, as you suppose. It's only nine in the morning! No, this is what was spoken by the prophet Joel: "In the last days, God says, I will pour out my Spirit on all people. Your sons and daughters will prophesy, your young men will see visions, your old men will dream dreams. Even on my servants, both men and women, I will pour out my Spirit in those days, and they will prophesy.

I will show wonders in the heavens above and signs on the earth below, blood and fire and billows of smoke. The sun will be turned to darkness and the moon to blood before the coming of the great and glorious day of the Lord. And everyone who calls on the name of the Lord will be saved."

Just think of what it was like on the day of Pentecost when the Holy Spirit blazed a trail from heaven to here on earth! For all believers, this was the greatest day that has ever been besides Christ's birth, death, and, resurrection!

Could the Holy Spirit come into our churches today exactly the way He did in the upper room? Could He make such a grand entrance as back then and blow open the doors with a mighty wind, and place tongues of fire upon each person there? Could He fill each person, including children with His power, resulting in everyone speaking in other tongues (speaking languages other than their native language)? The scriptures say that this was the evidence that they were filled with the Holy Spirit. Could He give the gifts of the Spirit to all those who are there so they can go forth and do the work of the ministry? Would some who would witness His arrival and ministry consider it out of order and not of God?

These hundred and twenty disciples were earnestly waiting for Him to come. Jesus had already explained that He would send the Holy Spirit for all believers to receive power to become witnesses in all the earth. They understood that they needed Him to come and they were willing to wait on Him to arrive. Some scholars say they waited approximately 10 days. When the Holy Spirit did finally arrive, not only was He loud and noisy but, so was the crowd! They all prophesied and worshiped so much that they appeared drunk to the people in the streets who heard them.

Let me ask this question. Might we be afraid, in some of our churches, that if we let the Holy Spirit loose to do whatever He wants to, He might do something akin to what happened at Pentecost? He might cause those who want more of Him to speak in other tongues or start dancing around and praising and worshiping Him, bringing confusion to the order of service. Some folks might become so undignified that they may get out of their seats or start standing in the aisles! Some believe that, if we can't be certain if what we see going on is fake or real, it's best not to allow any of it. There is a fear that if we cannot see and hear everything going on in that atmosphere then we are better off if we avoid it altogether. What if someone starts prophesying and it is totally off track, and not of God at all, and causes someone to believe a lie? We can't take that chance.

It is true that you can't be sure that everything done in the name of the Holy Spirit is legitimate or ordained or initiated by *Him*. Some people can and will go overboard or operate in error and mishandle the gifts of the Spirit. Unfortunately, the same can be said about some evangelists, prophets, pastors, ministers, elders, deacons, and other leaders. Some mishandle the word of God and take advantage of God's people. We still, however, believe that God ordained those offices and set them in place over the church as spoken in Ephesians 4:11-12 (KJV):

> *And He gave some, apostles; and some, prophets; and some, evangelists; and some, pastors and teachers;* "For the perfecting of the saints, for the work of the ministry, for the edifying of the body of Christ".

We are not going to get rid of these God-ordained offices in the church because of what some false apostles, prophets, evangelists, pastors, and teachers have done in sin and error. Should we limit the freedom of the Holy Spirit to move in our churches and in our personal lives because of the possibility that some saints might miss it and need correcting? Do you throw out the baby with the bathwater and ban everything because some folks get into the wrong doctrine or behavior? That's why we need those wonderful five-fold ministries in the church to edify the body of Christ – to rebuke when needed and reprove for the perfecting of the saints. We need perfecting and direction as we mature and grow in practicing the freedom and liberty we find in the presence of God. We need that liberty now more than ever in the body of Christ. We need the freedom and encouragement from our leaders to reach out to God unashamedly and passionately as they also teach us what is right and proper to do before the Lord and what is not. Let them teach the body of Christ how to passionately pursue the glory of the Lord and how to dwell in His glory. Let us focus on the King and the Kingdom He wants us to establish on the earth. And when the Holy Spirit says we are done, our hearts will be prepared for the washing of the water by the Word of God. Our hearts will be grounded to receive those seeds and they will grow and flourish!

What is more important to you – to be changed and transformed in the presence of God, or to leave the church and carry back home the same hurts, unforgiveness, anguish, pain, sickness, poverty, and disease? Would you rather stand in his presence of the Lord and choose not to acknowledge Him or honor him as King of Kings and Lord of Lords? Would you refuse Him the accolades that only a King deserves – shouts of praise and adoration, bowing before Him, lifting up shouts of joys, clapping, and singing with exuberance? Would you prefer to maintain your dignity and posture as He enters the room as though He is just some ordinary man? I hope not.

Is God real to you or is He a culmination of Bible stories, fables, and tales?

Is God real to you or is He a culmination of Bible stories, fables, and tales? Is He your heavenly Father and creator of all things or do you come to church because you want to be a good person, or for other reasons? What do your praise and worship reveal about you?

If you want to surrender more of your heart and life to the Lord, you can do that right now! It takes the surrender of your will over to the Holy Spirit of God, giving Him permission to rule over your soul rather than your soul ruling over you. Your born-again spirit knows who God is and when it is in control, it will lead you to acknowledge and worship the Lord. Likewise, when your soul is in charge, it wants to exalt *you* instead of God. It will keep you in pride and it will always want to be on the *throne* of your heart instead of God.

If you are truly ready to surrender your will then it won't take a one-time prayer to get there. You have to *daily* build up your spiritual muscles to control your soul. You have to "feed" your spirit. Your spirit is not like your body. You can't feed your spirit natural food and drink because it doesn't consume that. Your spirit receives nourishment from the word of God (truth and revelation from God Himself), prayer (communion and fellowship with God), and abiding in His presence (talking to Him, ministering to Him, talking about

Him). Whenever you do these things, the Holy Spirit is present as the mediator or go-between to fill up your spirit with the revelation of the Word of God as you read or study it. He will also be present as you pray to the Father and He will reveal to your spirit what the Father says and what His will is.

There are many ways to abide in God's presence. As you practice them, the Holy Spirit will be the conduit to bring you into the presence of God and help you to remain there in fellowship with the Father or Jesus or Himself!

It's simple – the more you spend time practicing these things, the more you will want to surrender your will to God; the more real God becomes; the more you will want to spend time with Him; and the more you will want to worship Him. My friend, you will care less about what others think because His love and power are operating in your life and will become more important than anything or anyone else! You won't be *ashamed* to worship the Father, Son, and the Holy Spirit. Your shame will leave you when you truly know that you owe your very life to Jesus who rescued you from eternal death in hell. When you *know what great love it took for Jesus to die for you and for the Father to send His only Son on your behalf,* you will not have trouble praising Him. It won't be a struggle, my friend.

As your spirit becomes stronger through your study of the Word of God, spending time in prayer, and communing in God's presence, your spirit will take over and it will, it must worship God!

5

A Heart Willing to Repent

When I look back over my life, I can recall over the years how I attended church regularly unaware I had never repented of my sins and given my life to the Lord.

At a very early age, I was sent to Sunday school by my parents. It was during that time I learned that, on Sunday mornings, attending church was what you were supposed to do. Back then, in the 1960s, many of our neighbors and friends attended church regularly. It was very common decades ago, unlike today.

As I child, I enjoyed Sunday school, seeing my friends and learning Bible stories, and singing songs. I especially loved attending Vacation Bible School (VBS) at our local church once school was out for the summer. It was usually held in June or July for two weeks. Even children who didn't go to church regularly during the year would come out for VBS. The crafts we made and the closing festivities on the last day were a lot of fun. I do not doubt that those early years of my life helped shape my understanding of who God was. As a young child, I believed that not only did God exist, but He expected everyone to believe in Him, and to do good and not evil. It was many years later, in my adulthood that I finally understood that believing in God and being a good person was not enough to save me from hell, give me eternal life, and grant me forgiveness of my sins.

I came to view those years of attending church faithfully as akin to paying premiums on a life insurance policy. The only difference was I thought of it as a church-going policy that would grant me entrance into heaven and even elevate me to some degree before God when I stood before Him someday. I thought of myself as basically a good person who at least set aside time to go to church when so many other folks never did. I might have been partying the night before or engaged in some ungodly activities during the week but, I still went to church to pay my respects (or so I thought). I made sure I paid on my church-going policy!

It seems ridiculous now as I reminisce about those days. I am certain, however, I was not the only person who lived my life that way or who thought that way. Many church members are living that way today. I was an usher in my church, a member of the choir and I participated in many other ministries over the years. There are too many to mention here but, I wasn't saved. Many times, I prayed and asked God to forgive me for my sins (especially on a

Sunday morning after whatever transpired the night before). Unfortunately, I never REPENTED of my sins. I felt bad about my sin but, my nature was carnal.

Once I left the church after a service, in a matter of time, I forgot all about how bad I felt, and I simply did it all over again. If there wasn't a church, a preacher, or someone to remind me of my lifestyle and sin, I didn't even feel bad about it. That's why it's not enough to just believe in Christ and say the sinner's prayer. I must have said the sinner's prayer hundreds of times over the years at the end of a church service without any change in my life and my heart. You see, I did not repent.

Many people believe that baptism alone, whether you are young or old, gives you salvation and eternal life but, it does not. Baptism *is important* as a public witness and demonstration that you have chosen to follow Jesus and that your sins have been "washed" away through repentance. It is supposed to signify that you are turning away from your old sinful life and you are being cleansed to start a new life of righteousness in God. The scriptures clearly tell us in Matthew Chapter 3:1-6 that both the confession of sin and repentance is necessary to receive salvation:

> "In those days, John the Baptist came preaching in the wilderness of Judea, and saying, "Repent, for the kingdom of heaven is at hand!" For this is He who was spoken

> *of by the prophet Isaiah, saying: "The voice of One crying in the wilderness: 'Prepare the way of the Lord; Make His paths straight.'" Now John Himself was clothed in camel's hair, with a leather belt around His waist; and His food was locusts and wild honey. Then Jerusalem, all Judea, and all the region around the Jordan went out to Him and were baptized by Him in the Jordan" (KJV)*

Many people believe that baptism alone, whether you are young or old, gives you salvation and eternal life but, it does not.

John the Baptist made it clear to everyone who heard him preach that they must **repent** for the kingdom of God is at hand. Everyone who heeded his warning and chose to repent was then baptized by John. It was their repentance that then compelled them to want to be baptized. Baptism without true repentance does not give you salvation. The scripture says that they confessed their sins and he baptized them.

When someone repents, their heart is contrite and sorrowful for the life they had lived, and they want no more of it. They know in their heart that they are a sinner and need a Savior, just as we knew when we accepted Christ and as we know this moment if we have not repented. They want to change; they want to be clean; they want to be whole; they want a new life!

Have you ever repented and confessed your sins to the Father and changed the way you have been living?

Have you ever repented and confessed your sins to the Father and changed the way you have been living? It doesn't matter how often you grace the doors of the church or listen to praise music or TV evangelists, or good preaching, or even read your Bible. It doesn't matter if you give offerings regularly, or you partner with ministries or charities. You may be the most generous person you know always helping others in need. You might even consider yourself a moral or socially responsible person, and that may be true, but that is not enough to receive salvation and eternal life in heaven. Romans 3:23 (NKJV) states, *"For all have sinned, and come short of the glory of God;"* That includes you! We ALL have something we need forgiveness for and we must repent of.

Once the gospel has been shared with you and you comprehend it, you must make a life-changing decision. Do you want Christ, salvation, and the holy life more than you want the sin in your life that has you bound or that you may even enjoy? What about the relationships, issues, habits you are involved in that you know do not please God? Are you going to try to hold on to them with one hand and grab hold to Christ with the other? You can't. You have to be willing to endure the consequences that may come if you choose to follow Christ. You may lose money, friends, loved ones, opportunities, or even your reputation but, I believe you will never, never regret it.

Jesus gives you this promise, as Matthew 19:29 (KJV) states:

> *"And everyone who has left houses or brothers or sisters or father or mother or wife or children or lands, for My name's sake, shall receive a hundredfold, and inherit eternal life. But many who are first will be last, and the last first".*

There's even more good news. You don't have to depend on your strength to break free from the sin in your life! Jesus has set you free by His death on the cross. The Holy Spirit is waiting for you to decide in your heart to repent and to confess your sins to the Father. Once you do, you permit Him to quicken your spirit on the inside so that it takes authority over your fleshly and carnal desires. He will be with you and inside of you! You will be empowered with the authority to overcome all the schemes and plans of the enemy for your life! The Holy Spirit will also reveal God's word to you so can confess that word over your life and command the devil to flee! You will have victory through Christ Jesus who loved you and gave Himself as a ransom for you! You have heaven, eternity with righteousness, peace, and joy in the Holy Spirit to gain! You have death, hell, and the grave to lose!

A new life of freedom awaits you now because your new repented nature will hunger for more of Jesus. The Word of God will become more alive than you've ever known! The same scriptures you've heard, perhaps for years, will suddenly become alive to you. You will feel as though you understand them for the first time because the Holy Spirit will reveal them to your Spirit, which was once dead but is now alive. You will have a greater sensitivity to the Holy Spirit like never before. The same songs the choir has sung for years will sound different and move your heart. The words to the songs will have greater meaning to you. You may have been moved many times before, stirred by the praise and worship in your service but, you will begin to experience a deeper response to the Lord... beyond your emotions... you will worship Him in Spirit and truth. You will be changed from the inside out because your spirit will be one with the Holy Spirit. You will commune with Him beyond your feelings. You will *know* Him.

In the past, you may have left church on a high because of good preaching, good singing, and good fellowship and it left you feeling so encouraged and willing to make some changes in your life. As the week rolled by, the message and the music, and the fellowship slowly faded away as you returned to your normal activities and lifestyle. Somehow, none of it penetrated deeply enough in your soul to make a permanent change in direction for your life. It touched the surface of your heart but never penetrated it and changed it. With the Holy Spirit now living on the inside of you, you will see life spring forth in areas of your life that have been dormant and unchanged. You will not only understand what needs to change in your life but, the Holy Spirit will affect that change because you are willing!

As you worship, pray and read the word of God, you will be so grateful that He pursued you and you said yes to Him! You will experience the ability to worship any time and any place because your Spirit has an online connection with heaven! God bless you as you enjoy this new life of freedom from sin, condemnation, and the bondage of the enemy!

6

A Heart Yielded to the Holy Spirit

I want to challenge you, no matter what the standard or example of worship is at your church. You should never be ashamed to praise and worship your dear Savior Jesus Christ. You should never fear the faces of men and women nor their opinion of you. The only opinions you should value are those of your heavenly Father, your Savior Jesus, and your helper the Holy Spirit.

What is the big deal anyway about how you worship or behave in public services? Well, if I asked you whether you agree that something is wrong with a married couple or a couple in love who never laugh together, smile at one another, hold hands or show any affection, you would say a resounding "yes, of course!". You would expect, that if they truly care for one another then something should be evident in their actions toward one another. Their body language should show that their relationship is more than one of an acquaintance or just a friendship. I'm not saying that they should behave this way all the time. If you happen to spend time with them regularly, then you should be able to tell that they enjoy one another's companionship and they care for one another. Even the way they look at one another should give some clue! In fact, if they happen to tell you they don't sleep together, eat together, live together or spend any time together, you would assume that something must be wrong with their marriage or relationship. You would question how much they love one another because, by nature, a good healthy relationship results in affection and tenderness. A couple in a committed and loving relationship tries to spend time together whenever possible.

Let's apply that example to our relationship with Christ because it is a personal relationship. Have you ever thought of it that way? Do you know that even though you and I are human beings we can be in a relationship with almighty God? We can fellowship with a deity. We really can. That is all God has ever wanted from mankind. That is why Adam was created and then Eve. When they sinned against God and received judgment, God the Father sent Jesus, His only begotten Son to come to the earth and live a sinless life and die on the cross for our sins. Jesus obeyed the Father so we could be restored to a loving relationship with Him.

Are you in a committed relationship with Christ Jesus? What do I mean? If you have accepted Him as Savior, that's great and is the first step but, the next step is to receive the baptism of the Holy Spirit. You may ask, how does that happen and why would I need to do that? Baptism in the Holy Spirit or, as it is sometimes referred to as being filled with the Holy Spirit, is a vital and transformative experience that every born again believer must receive to experience the *fullness* of the power, presence, and victory that Jesus died on the cross to give us. When that wonderful salvation was given and you became a Christian, the Holy Spirit came to live inside of you. You were in a sense resurrected to a new life just as Christ was resurrected after dying on the cross at Calvary. Here is how the Bible explains it,

> *Romans 6:4 (NLT) states, "For we died and were buried with Christ by baptism. And just as Christ was raised from the dead by the glorious power of the Father, now we also may live new lives."*

When we received Christ as Savior, our old nature was buried with baptism just as Christ physically was buried. When Christ was raised by the glorious power of the Holy Spirit, we were raised into a new life by the same Holy Spirit that now lives inside of us. We left our old sinful life in the

> **The Holy Spirit was sent to equip the saints to rule and reign and overcome the kingdom of darkness.**

grave and there is more! Now that we have a new nature, Jesus sent the Holy Spirit to give us power, spiritual gifts, utterances of other tongues, and revelation so we can destroy the works of darkness in our age and generation throughout the whole earth! The Holy Spirit was sent to equip the saints to rule and reign and overcome the kingdom of darkness. He is here to make us ready for every battle to come and to win them!

> Ephesians 1:4 (NLT) states, "The Spirit is God's guarantee that He will give us the inheritance He promised and that He has purchased us to be His own people" He did this so we would praise and glorify Him."

Jesus purchased us by dying on the cross so we could be God's own people. You are missing out on your inheritance if you reject the ministry of the Holy Spirit! Jesus didn't rescue you from hell and eternal damnation to leave you to fight the powers of darkness all alone. You and I, in our own power, are no match for the devil but, the power of the Holy Spirit working through us is more than the devil's match!

Kenneth Erwin Hagin explains the work of the Holy Spirit in this brief excerpt. He was an American preacher known as the "father of the modern faith movement," Rev. Hagin was a dynamic preacher, teacher, and prophet. His teachings and books are filled with vivid stories that show God's power and truth working in his life and the lives of others.[1]

In His book *"Why Tongues",* Kenneth E. Hagin shares the following:

> *"There is a work of the Holy Spirit in the new birth, but that is not called receiving the Holy Spirit—that is called being born-again, receiving Eternal Life. There is an experience following salvation called receiving, or being filled with the Holy Spirit. When the apostles at Jerusalem heard of the wonderful things God had done through Philip's ministry in Samaria, they sent Peter and John to lay hands on the new converts that they might receive the Holy Spirit."* [2]

It is important to understand here that, when you accepted Christ, the Holy Spirit orchestrated the "new birth" on the inside of you. He was fully involved and He is the one who helped you transition from the darkness of your selfish and sinful nature to a new life and a new nature as His dear son or daughter. He washed you clean. He gave you a new mind and new motivations and desires for what is holy. He made you brand new! That is such an amazing and incredible miracle that took place. It is the greatest miracle that could have happened to you.

Now, after you have been saved, there is a second miracle that He wants to release into your life. This experience is called being filled with the Holy Spirit or being "baptized in the Holy Spirit." It is evidenced by speaking in tongues just as the early apostles did once they received the Holy Spirit in the Upper Room at Jerusalem. Jesus told them to go and wait there until the Holy Spirit arrived:

> *Then He said, "When I was with you before, I told you that everything written about me in the law of Moses and the prophets and in the Psalms must be fulfilled." Then He opened their minds to understand the Scriptures. And He said, "Yes, it was written long ago that the Messiah would suffer and die and rise from the dead on the third day. It was also written that this message would be proclaimed in the authority of His name to all the nations, beginning in Jerusalem: 'There is forgiveness of sins for all who repent.' You are witnesses of all these things. "And now I will send the Holy Spirit, just as my Father promised. But stay here in*

the city until the Holy Spirit comes and fills you with power from heaven" (Luke 24:44-49 NLT).

Jesus would not send the apostles out to the nations to declare His name until the Holy Spirit had come to fill them. They needed to be filled with 'power' from on high to do the work that every believer is called to do. The Holy Spirit was not only sent to the apostles of the early church. He is sent to you and me today. He is necessary for you and me today to fulfill our purpose as born-again believers. We need His power! We need the gifts of the Spirit that He has for all believers.

The Holy Spirit is truly a gift to the body of Christ. His importance and the manifestation of His gifts have been documented through many famous and infamous pastors, evangelists, prophets, and teachers through the centuries. One such evangelist who operated in spiritual gifts in the 18th century was George Whitefield (1714-1770). George Whitefield, together with John Wesley and Charles Wesley, founded the Methodist movement. An Anglican evangelist and the leader of Calvinistic Methodists, he was the most popular preacher of the Evangelical Revival in Great Britain and the Great Awakening in America. [3]

Listen to what George Whitefield states about the Holy Spirit,

"Judge ye, then, my brethren, whether it is not high time for the true ministers of Jesus Christ who have been themselves made partakers of this heavenly gift, to lift up their voices like a trumpet, and, if they would not have those souls perish for which the Lord Jesus has shed His precious blood to declare, with all boldness, that the Holy Spirit is the common privilege and portion of all believers in all ages; and that we also, as well as the first Christians, must receive the Holy Spirit ere we can be truly called the children of God." 4

Kenneth E. Hagin expounds below on His experiences with the Holy Spirit and speaking tongues:

1 Corinthians 14:4 (KJV) states,"Paul encouraged the Corinthian Christians to continue the practice of speaking with other tongues in their worship of God. He also encouraged them to speak in tongues in their individual prayer life as a means of spiritual edification or building up. The Bible says, "He that speaketh in an unknown tongue edifieth Himself . . .". Paul also stated in 1 Corinthians 14:14, "For if I pray in an unknown tongue, MY SPIRIT PRAYETH, but my understanding is unfruitful." Notice He said, "My spirit prays." Corinthians 14:14 in the Amplified

Bible reads, "My spirit [by the Holy Spirit within me] prays . . . ." God is a Spirit. When you pray in tongues, your spirit is in direct contact with God, who is a Spirit. When you speak in tongues, you are talking to Him by divine, supernatural means. [5]

The Holy Spirit and His ministry are often misunderstood, even by the body of Christ. Some believe that speaking in other tongues, the gifts of the Spirit, and the Holy Spirit Himself is simply a doctrine only followed by certain denominations. Others believe He has little or no relevance in their church community despite His role throughout the Bible. Some believe the Holy Spirit only appeared in the Old Testament days and does not exist on the earth today. There are even Christians who have been filled with the Holy Spirit who rarely talk to Him, pray in their heavenly language (tongues), or acknowledge that He lives on the inside of them.

The truth is that some folks are afraid of the Holy Spirit. The truth is that some folks are afraid of the Holy Spirit. Yes, afraid. They have heard or have seen people do strange things under the "influence" of the Holy Spirit. They ask, "What is that gibberish those people are speaking? Why are they making those loud and funny noises?" I can relate to that because I have previously thought the same thing. I even witnessed folks shake or fall to the ground! I asked, "Why would any "normal" person want to engage in that kind of behavior? What could that possibly accomplish? It is just a bunch of theatrics." I thought that what my denomination believed and practiced was the totality of who God was and what He does. We were taught about "supernatural" events in the old and new testament but, I believed that was only in manifestation in those days. I thought that because all of those disciples, prophets, ordinary folks, and Jesus were long gone, so were those miracles. Not true.

When the Holy Spirit lives on the inside of you, He won't make you do anything against your will! He won't take over your mind and make you go crazy as some believe. He won't take over your mouth and make you speak like a lunatic. And He certainly will not attack you and make you suddenly lose control of your body. What we have seen happen to people that appear to mimic these things was simply the power of the Holy Spirit as it touches and ministers to someone.

There have been revivals in the United States that have been known, not only for great conversions of men and women to Jesus Christ but, also for the notable miracles and manifestations of the Holy Spirit. In the Azusa Street Revival, in Los Angeles, CA, between 1906 and 1915, William J. Seymour presided over meetings where physical healings took place, the gift of tongues was in operation and members and guests were slain in the spirit (they became weak and fell to the ground). The participants were criticized by some secular media and Christian theologians for behaviors considered to be outrageous and unorthodox, especially at the time. Today, the revival is considered by historians to be the primary catalyst for the spread of Pentecostalism in the 20th century. [6]

Throughout history, the Holy Spirit has continued to demonstrate His power in the same way. Whether it was the Levitical priests who ministered in old testament days within the temple of God and could not stand when the cloud of God's presence came; or Moses who saw God's glory; or David who danced for joy; or Saul of Tarsus who fell off His horse at the sound of the Lord's voice, the Holy Spirit ministers in power that, at times, causes our mortal bodies to lose strength to stand. Yet, it is nothing to be feared. We need His power in our lives. We need His guidance. We need His comfort and peace. We need Him!

How do you receive the baptism of the Holy Spirit? Just ask in faith believing that it will be done. When you received Jesus as your Savior, you believed that if you repented of your sins and asked Jesus into your heart that you would be saved. The same faith it took to receive salvation is necessary to receive the baptism of the Holy Spirit. Faith is the catalyst. It sets it all into motion. Your faith is your permission to the Holy Spirit to come and inhabit your inward man or your spirit. He will come in, with His power and with housewarming gifts. What do I mean?

Bishop Wellington Boone, in His book "Holy Spirit is My Friend", gives this encouragement to believers as they seek the baptism in the Holy Spirit. He is the founder and chief prelate of the Fellowship of International Churches, a cross-cultural, global network of bishops, pastors, missionaries, and Bible-based churches and Bible schools.[7]

> *"Your prayer language may not come immediately. Some believers ask Jesus to baptize them in the Holy Spirit and speak in tongues as an instant manifestation, but it is not always the case. The disciples' experienced the Baptism with the Holy Spirit and spoke in tongues at Pentecost in a moment of time. However, that moment did not come without effort. They had first sought to obey Jesus and follow Him with commitment and sacrifice. When will the gift come and what should you do while you are waiting? Keep seeking God and reading what He said in His Word. Spend time in Christian churches and other Christian environments where expressions of His miracles and manifestation are welcome. Fulfill the Great Commission."* [8]

If you desire more understanding of the baptism of the Holy Spirit, read Acts 2 in the Bible about the arrival of the Holy Spirit to the early church. Also, read the following accounts of the ministry of the Holy Spirit in the Bible (John 14:26; John 1:33; John 7:39; Luke 1:15: Luke 1:41; Luke 1:67; Luke 2:40; Acts 4:8; Acts 4:31; Acts 9:17; Acts 13:9; Acts 13:15; Ephesians 5:18).

7

A Heart that Understands the Role of the Holy Spirit in a Christian's life

1 Corinthians 12:1-11 (NIV) states,

"Now about the gifts of the Spirit, brothers, and sisters, I do not want you to be uninformed. You know that when you were pagans, somehow or other you were influenced and led astray to mute idols. Therefore, I want you to know that no one who is speaking by the Spirit of God says, "Jesus be cursed," and no one can say, "Jesus is Lord," except by the Holy Spirit. There are different kinds of gifts, but the same Spirit distributes them. There are different kinds of service, but the same Lord. There are different kinds of working, but in all of them and in everyone it is the same God at work.

Now to each one, the manifestation of the Spirit is given for the common good. To one there is given through the Spirit a message of wisdom, to another a message of knowledge by means of the same Spirit, to another faith by the same Spirit, to another

> *gifts of healing by that one Spirit, to another miraculous power, to another prophecy, to another distinguishing between Spirits, to another speaking in different kinds of tongues, and to still another the interpretation of tongues. All these are the work of one and the same Spirit, and He distributes them to each one, just as He determines".*

In these passages above, we see that the Holy Spirit plays a role when we are converted (born again) and later when He gives us the *gifts of the Spirit* as a part of our inheritance as believers in the Messiah Jesus. We need the Holy Spirit's help to be able to call Jesus Lord. He must quicken our Spirit by filling our Spirit with Himself so it can understand and know that *Jesus is the Messiah* and that we are lost and in need of a Savior. How amazing that Jesus gave Himself fully to die on the cross and suffer the punishment that we deserve. The Holy Spirit gives Himself fully to reveal who Jesus is so we can accept the sacrifice Jesus made.

The Holy Spirit takes up residence on the inside of us once we make Jesus Lord of our lives.

The Holy Spirit connects our spirit, soul, and body back in fellowship again with the Father. He reveals

Jesus to us so we can call Jesus Lord. That's why no man who curses Jesus has the Holy Spirit and every man who calls Him Lord does!

The Holy Spirit takes up residence on the inside of us once we make Jesus Lord of our lives. From that point on, He becomes our guide! He is our guide into all truth. Now a guide can lead you to places you don't know how to get to on your own but, you must be willing to follow Him. Are you willing to follow where the Holy Spirit gently leads? He is truly gentle and tender. He will never force you to go where he leads or do anything without your surrender to Him.

How do you know he's leading, you say? You will know because you want His help. You are asking for His help in prayer and petition so He comes and you can sense His presence. You may be reading the Bible and you will sense His presence or have an awareness of peace, love, or both. You may notice that any anxiety you had is gone because His word or prayer or meditation about the Father, Jesus, or the Holy Spirit has changed your state of mind to a sweet loving reverence for them all. Even in worship, you will find the Holy Spirit's participation because His Spirit now lives in you as a born-again believer. You can know how the Father and Jesus feel because the Holy Spirit is the translator living inside of you. The Father and the Son can know how you feel because the Holy Spirit is one with both of them.

He opens the frequency channel from your spirit to God!

He came into your heart (Spirit) to dwell there and to reveal who Jesus Christ is. He opens the frequency channel from your spirit to God! He is the *transmitter*; He is the *interpreter* for your spirit of all the Lord is sharing with you and what your response should be to God. He causes your soul (mind, will, emotions) to receive understanding from Him (the Holy Spirit) to know what the will of God is for you.

You play a role in whether the Holy Spirit can do all He wants to in your life. You must decide to yield to that understanding, truth, and embrace it as a decision of your will as you live for the Lord. The more you yield to the Holy Spirit, the less you are controlled by your emotions, and the more you think like God.

One of God's many attributes is peace. God maintains that state of mind and thought because He has nothing to fear. He isn't afraid of anything in the present, nor afraid of what tomorrow will bring. He created tomorrow and your destiny is to spend your future with Him throughout all eternity. God isn't worried about anything or anyone, hallelujah! The more you think like God, the more you too will walk in peace.

The more you and I yield to the Holy Spirit then we will know that we have nothing to fear because the Lord fights our battles.

The more you and I yield to the Holy Spirit then we will know that we have nothing to fear because the Lord fights our battles. The Holy Spirit reveals these truths to us about God the Father and Jesus. The Bible says the following about the Holy Spirit in John 16:13 (AMP). Jesus explained to the disciples that once He departed earth, after the resurrection, he would return to the Father in heaven and send the Holy Spirit.

"But when He, the Spirit of Truth, comes, He will guide you into all the truth [full and complete truth]. For He will not speak on His own initiative, but He will speak whatever He hears [from the Father—the message regarding the Son], and He will disclose to you what is to come [in the future]".

The Holy Spirit will not speak of His own initiative. He is here on the earth to speak on behalf of the Father, relaying all to us, to encourage us and exalt Jesus our great high priest, redeemer, and King of Kings. The Holy Spirit speaks to us about what He hears God the Father and Jesus say. He decrees and declares the messages of God to mankind. He carries out God's obligation to the covenant that exists between God and mankind. God is a covenant-keeping God. He never fails in keeping His promises to mankind though we do. He is long-suffering and so patient and kind toward us. He has kept His promises to Israel His chosen people, to the earth He created and to mankind He created. The Holy Spirit oversees and ensures that the promises of God are carried out on the earth. He is the executor of the covenant.

The Holy Spirit will tell you what is to come in the future. The Holy Spirit will tell you what is to come in the future. He will reveal the secret things of God to you. Because, as a born-again believer, He has come to dwell inside of you within your Spirit, you can hear Him speaking, leading, and guiding you as a witness to you of the things to come that you need to know, so you can make sound decisions. It is the Holy one living on the inside of you that speaks to you through thoughts, a sense of awareness of what is to come, or by allowing you to see or hear about what is to come. He can reveal the future to you either inwardly by speaking to your mind by feelings, or emotions, or within your spirit. He can also reveal it outwardly. If outwardly then He will use your natural senses and He may show you signs or allow you to see or hear information that is a clue to the future and what you must do. He chooses which way to guide you that is best for you.

He equips the saints with the power to overcome weaknesses in the flesh that would cause them to sin. He equips them with weapons of authority and power over all of the power of the evil one. He leads them in the paths of righteousness and holiness for He is holiness. He is Spirit and He is holy. Holiness is one of the attributes of the Godhead and so is love. The Holy Spirit demonstrates both.

He has come to restore all things back to God's original plan and state. That original plan was that God wanted a people who would, by nature do what is just and right, pure, and perfect. They would love unconditionally and willingly. This great love put into their nature would cause them to have to give it to others. Unconditional love needs an object of that love. Just as we were the object of God's love, we, in turn, would be fruitful and multiply and replenish the earth and share our love with those yet to be created. That is still God's plan.

Jesus came first to provide a way for us to be restored to our former relationship with the Father that Adam and Eve enjoyed before they fell into sin. Now the Holy Spirit has been sent to show us how to walk in that freedom from bondage and sin that Christ purchased on our behalf. He must teach us how to walk and live righteously because our nature is to sin. That's why the scripture says that He will guide us into all truth! That is why we can have victory over our sinful nature because we can exchange our unrighteousness for Jesus' righteousness, and we have a helper and guide (the Holy Spirit) to lead us through the journey of life and teach us all things! Therefore, the scriptures declare the following in 1 John 4:4 (AMP):

> *"Little children (believers, dear ones), you are of God and you belong to Him and have [already] overcome them [the agents of the antichrist]; because He who is in you is greater than He (satan) who is in the world [of sinful mankind]".*

Yes, the Holy Spirit living on the inside of you as a born-again believer is greater (stronger) than your sinful nature. He is greater than every fiery dart and evil work of darkness in the earth that would try to control you or come against you. God Himself has come to dwell on the inside of you! God who is love, light, and power and has taken up residence on the inside of you! You have the power on the inside of you to overcome every addiction in your life. You have the power on the inside to free you of anything holding you captive. It doesn't matter what it is or how long you have been bound by it.

Even now, if you would call on the name of Jesus and declare your freedom and liberty from the struggles you have contended with, the Holy Spirit will hear and come to your rescue. It may be drug addictions, sex addictions, pornography, violence, anger, lust, abuse, perversion, premarital sex, homosexuality, adultery, hatred, unforgiveness, rejection, depression, suicide, offenses, and others. Let the spirit of the most high God come and bring healing and restoration to you that Jesus paid for on the cross. Let the Holy Spirit do the work He was commissioned to do by Jesus Christ. Allow Him to work on the inside of your soul and restore your body, soul, and mind. Yield to Him and allow Him to lead you into all righteousness as He can do. If you give Him your will, He will give you in exchange a new desire for the things of God. He will give you a new nature that wants to please God and that understands that the love of the Father is so unfathomable that it compels us to want to please Him. When you know how much the Father loves you and you know how much Jesus sacrificed for you then you will know you are so very cherished by God. You are so precious to Him; so very precious. The Lord Himself sings over you with rejoicing! Zephaniah 3:17 (NIV) says,

> "The Lord your God is with you, the Mighty Warrior who saves. He will take great delight in you; in His love He will no longer rebuke you, but will rejoice over you with singing".

Imagine that! The Lord your God takes such great delight in you that He will not remember your past sins once you have repented but, He will rejoice over you with singing! Yes, God laughs and sings. We were made in His image so, if we laugh and sing, so does He. When we call upon the name of the Lord, as we seek righteousness, then it delights the Father. He wants us back into the family! He wants us washed clean by the blood of Jesus. He wants us to come out of the darkness and into His marvelous light. He wants to bestow upon us all the rights and privileges that a son and daughter have been given. Yes, it brings Him joy, great joy!

For those who would turn away from God and choose their way, He knows the heartache, turmoil, and defeat waiting for anyone who rejects Him. He has to stand by and allow it to take place because He cannot force anyone to repent and be saved. It grieves the Father to watch His creation suffer here on earth and then, after death, be condemned to spend an eternity suffering in hell. That same love that rejoices over us when we have been brought out of captivity to our sins and is the same love that sorrows when we are a slave to sin. If we can experience sorrow and rejection, then so can God and He does.

> **He didn't create us so He could send as many souls to hell as possible. He created us so He could fill heaven with as many saints as possible.**

He didn't create us so He could send as many souls to hell as possible. He created us so He could fill heaven with as many saints as possible. He sent the Holy Spirit here to be our "Spirit of truth" tour guide on this journey through life so that our final destination would be heaven! You and I can't make it there without Him. We need the power of the Holy Spirit to come and illuminate our way.

Proverbs 16:25 (AMP) states, "There is a way which seems right to a man and appears straight before Him, But its end is the way of death".

The Holy Spirit was sent to show us the right path and how to make the right decisions. Making "right" decisions is the same as living "righteously." There is a way or a path that seems right to follow but it leads to destruction (Proverbs 14:12). You and I can't see what's up ahead on the road we are traveling on. We can't see the dead ends we are approaching. We can't see the dangers lurking ahead. There are dark alleys with dangerous people waiting to attack but, there is one who knows *everything* that lies in wait for us. He is our precious protector and guide – the Holy Spirit.

If you will obey the leading of the Holy Spirit and value His advice, heed His warnings, follow His instructions, and be confident that whatever He does is in line with the Father's will, He will help you to avoid destruction and lead you down the chosen path that God has ordained for your life. Living this life without the hand of God to guide and protect you is like driving a car blindfolded and expecting to find your way safely to your destination. It's just not possible. Sooner or later you are going to crash! But, living a spirit-led life is such a wonderful adventure of pursuing and obtaining the promises of God; wrestling with the enemy and triumphing over Him through the blood of the lamb (Christ Jesus) and the Word of our testimony (Revelation 12:11); fighting the good fight of faith, which requires us to stand and believe the Word of God no matter how things look. We have a supreme advantage over the enemy – we have the Holy Spirit guiding us through the darkness and lighting the way with the truth. We don't have to be afraid of anything we have to face because we have the Holy Spirit on the inside of us. We only must look to Him for guidance; inquire of His wisdom and direction for our lives and He will intervene and guide the way. He is never, NEVER wrong! He will never lead you the wrong way.

Embrace the spirit-filled, spirit-led life. You begin by choosing not to lean unto your understanding but, lean on the understanding that comes from the Holy Spirit. That's step number one. Step two is to "practice His presence". Take the time, as much as possible, to get to know the Holy Spirit. He is a person. He is not an "it", nor a thing, not a thought, not a scary ghost but a person. God the Father is a person; God the Son (Jesus) is a person and so is the Holy Spirit. Just talk to Him like you would your best friend. He wants to be your best friend. That is why Jesus sent Him. Let Him take charge of your life. That means that before you act, consult Him. It also means that you choose to live holy because the "Holy" Spirit will not dwell inside of a filthy, unholy vessel. Does that mean that you must be perfect? No! It means that, if you desire to be holy and you are doing everything you can to live holy, He will help you to pursue holiness in every area of your life. Again – that is what He came for.

So, if you are a new Christian, the Bible says this –

2 Corinthians 5:17 (NKJV): "Therefore, if anyone is in Christ, He is a new creation; old things have passed away; behold, all things have become new".

The old things in your life are passed away and remembered no more. Everything about you has become new. On the outside, you may look the same but, you have been transformed on the inside! That's where the real change begins!

Even if you have just accepted Christ moments ago, you can start right now talking to the Holy Spirit and confessing your sins, yielding your heart and your life to Him. He is waiting to help you any time you call on Him. Now is a very good time to do just that!

Step three is spending time reading and understanding the Bible and the Holy Spirit, which will help your understanding. You may need to join a Bible study in the local church you are attending. If you have not yet joined a church, then ask the Holy Spirit to guide you to where He wants you to be. You need to be a part of a local church where you can study the word of God and grow in your understanding of how to live a holy life as a believer in Jesus Christ.

The word of God is like a seed that must be planted in fertile soil to grow and bring forth fruit that will remain. The Holy Spirit provides the light and fertilizer and water to make that seed (word of God) grow on the inside of you. He can till the ground of your heart and make it pliable and ready for the word to plant and yield a great harvest. He tends the garden of your heart so it will not harden or become stony ground or too dry and not fit for the word (seed to grow). He knows how and when to apply the right amount of sunshine, rain, and nutrients to keep the seed growing and stay healthy and vibrant until it's time for harvest.

Make it a priority to plant the seed of the word of God into your soul that has been made ready by the Holy Spirit to receive. Also, as you yield and give the Holy Spirit permission to tell you what to do, where to go, what to believe, what is righteous and what is unrighteous, how to forgive, how to love, and so on, then He can pluck up that old nature that doesn't belong in a born-again believer. He will, instead, plant in its place what does belong which is righteousness, peace, faith, and love.

You also need fellowship with other believers, and so the Lord wants to place you with a "spiritual family" in a local church. Don't wander around like a "spiritual" orphan and never join a church. Once you join one, be faithful to attend it regularly. If you are yielding your life to the Holy Spirit then I promise, He will guide you to be a faithful member of a church who hungers for the things of God.

Have you been preaching, teaching, and encouraging others while you have been privately struggling yourself to be hopeful and encouraged? You simply need to be filled with the Holy Spirit with the evidence of speaking in tongues and you need to learn to use your heavenly language daily to communicate to Him. At the end of this book, there are resources listed to help you understand more about the Holy Spirit's indwelling, infilling, and how to be baptized in the Holy Spirit. Perhaps, you did not know who the Holy Spirit is. His ministry is not only available to you but, it is vital to your growth and empowerment to overcome all the wiles of the devil! Please don't delay receiving this power from on high!

8

A Heart Free of Condemnation for Past Sins

Can you imagine for a few moments a Sunday morning service in progress in any Christian church within any part of the world? Imagine you can hear the songs being lifted harmoniously as musicians play and singers joyously praise and worship God? If you could hear the thoughts of some of the members there, you might be surprised to find that, although they are singing and seem to enjoy the service, they actually feel fear inside. Although they are actively participating in the service, their secret thoughts are reverberating around how miserably they have failed to obey God and follow His word during the previous week.

They may even feel condemnation from the devil who constantly follows them around and points out their weaknesses and their past sins. They have received Christ as Savior and they truly want to be in church. They also recognize their need for God but somehow, they don't understand or believe that Jesus has made them a new creature. All they can see is their failures before salvation and after salvation. They just don't understand that the power to live for Christ already dwells inside of them by the Holy Spirit. Jesus gave us forgiveness of sin we could never have obtained for ourselves.

The word of God explains it this way —

> *"In the past, you were dead because you sinned and fought against God. You followed the ways of this world and obeyed the devil. He rules the world, and His Spirit has power over everyone who doesn't obey God. Once we were also ruled by the selfish desires of our bodies and minds. We had made God angry, and we were going to be punished like everyone else. But God was merciful! We were dead because of our sins, but God loved us so much that He made us alive with Christ, and God's wonderful kindness is what saves you. God raised us from death to life with Christ Jesus, and He has given us a place beside Christ in heaven. God did this so that in the future world He could show how truly good and kind He is to us because of what Christ Jesus has done. You were saved by faith in God, who treats us much better than we deserve". This isn't something you have earned, so there is nothing you can brag about. God planned for us to do good things and to live as He has always wanted*

us to live. That's why He sent Christ to make us what we are." (Ephesians 2:1-10 CEV).

The scripture sums up it all! How can you fear judgment from God if you have repented of your sins and God has raised you from death (the old sinful life) to life?

God isn't sitting on high waiting for you to make another mistake so He can judge you.

Proverbs 24:16 (ESV) says, "for the righteous falls seven times and rises again, but the wicked stumble in times of calamity" Have you fallen this day? Yesterday? Last week? Repent and rise again!

There's no sin meter following you around and keeping track of how many things you do right and how many you do wrong. God isn't sitting on high waiting for you to make another mistake so He can judge you. Why would He have even bothered to send His dear, precious, only begotten Son to die for you so you could be rescued from death and eternal damnation? Would He do that and then watch and wait for you to fall and miss the mark? Do you imagine Him saying there's no hope for you? You just keep messing up. Does that make any sense that He would let His Son suffer for nothing if His blood could not free you from judgment? John 3:17 (KJV) explains it this way,

> For God sent not His Son into the world to condemn the world; but that the world through Him might be saved.

Jesus suffered, bled, and died in your place to pay the penalty of death you owed so why don't you believe that was enough? Don't fear the judgment of God because you sinned this week. Repent quickly when you sin and believe! The power of God you need to break the bondage and sin you struggle with comes in believing that you are walking in Jesus' righteousness and not on your own. When you said the sinner's prayer, you exchanged your unrighteousness for His righteousness. The Holy Spirit now works in your life to strengthen you to overcome all the power of the enemy.

You have a right to approach God in private and in the assembly of the saints and worship Him. If He brings something to your remembrance during worship that you should repent of then do so. Just realize that repenting and staying clean is going to be a regular practice in your walk with the Lord. Don't think that because you need to repent often that you are going to be condemned by God. David in the Bible had to repent many times and he wrote many verses in the Psalms about it. The apostles had to do it, along with the old patriarchs, and we have to do it.

> *Romans 8:1-5 (ESV) states, "There is therefore now no condemnation for those who are in Christ Jesus. For the law of the Spirit of life has set you free in Christ Jesus from the law of sin and death. For God has done what the law, weakened by the flesh, could not do. By sending His own Son in the likeness of sinful flesh and for sin, He condemned sin in the flesh, in order that the righteous requirement of the law might be fulfilled in us, who walk not according to the flesh but according to the Spirit".*

If you are in Christ Jesus, there should be no more condemnation! He has fulfilled the requirement of the law having lived a sinless, righteous life in our place and dying once on the cross for all those who will believe and accept His sacrifice.

The Amplified Bible puts it this way:

> *Romans 8:1 (AMP) says, "Therefore, there is now no condemnation [no guilty verdict, no punishment] for those*

> who are in Christ Jesus [who believe in Him as personal Lord and Savior]".

Do you believe in Jesus as your personal Lord and Savior? If so, then you should believe that there is no guilty verdict or punishment for you. There is no reason to expect God's wrath or His displeasure *unless you never intend to obey His commandments and submit your will to his.*

Henceforth, do not be afraid to approach the Lord in worship and prayer. In addition, do not receive the condemnation sent from that old deceiver, the devil. **Disregard your past sins if you have repented of them and you know that your heart desires to serve the Lord and obey His commandments.** You are qualified to serve the Lord and worship Him because His blood has washed you clean. He remembers your sins no more! You can come boldly to the throne of God not because you are so good and holy but because Jesus is the free gift of salvation.

9

A Heart Wanting More Than a Casual Relationship with God

Now that you've come out of darkness into His marvelous light, can you recall what it was like to live your life as you pleased? Were you totally independent of God, or simply without the knowledge that God was even real and had a plan for your life? Did your life feel as though you were living in a house without electricity all of your life not realizing that it is not normal or good to live in the dark? When all you have known your entire life is darkness and others around you are in the dark as well then that becomes the status quo.

Things changed when you were introduced to Jesus. Every dark place became illuminated with His warmth, His truth, and light. His light dispelled the dark places in your heart and your life. You began to see what you couldn't see before. You began to believe what you couldn't believe before. There was hope when before you had nothing but doubts and fears. You wanted Jesus and His truth to change your life. You knew you needed Him and His saving power. You wanted salvation. You wanted to be saved. Why did you need to be saved? Because you were drowning in sin and you understood that hell was your destination if you didn't repent. You knew it in the core of your being where your Spirit dwells.

Since you've accepted Christ as your personal Savior, maybe the journey hasn't been easy but, the peace has surpassed all understanding.

As you look back over your life since you have accepted Christ as your personal Savior, how much would you say you have grown as a Christian? Has it been a gradual but steady growth? Has it been rather slow but, you have grown nevertheless? Have you grown by leaps and bounds?

Maybe you weren't a churchgoer before you accepted Christ and now you are. Perhaps, you did attend church before salvation because you felt it was your duty or it was customary to do so for as long as you could remember. You may have been among those who were raised in the church, but you had never repented of your sins and asked Jesus to save you. Now you have.

There are some who had a genuine conversion and served God for a season but, at some point in their walk with Christ, they fell back into sin and turned away from Christ. Perhaps, none of these apply to you but, the question is, are you growing in your walk and journey with Christ now, or have you become stagnant? Are you comfortable with your Christian life as is and you don't desire an even closer relationship with Christ? Are you wondering, "What does this have to do with worship?" Good question.

You see, there is so much more to know about God and to enjoy as you fellowship with him! Remove the limitations in your thinking that what you have experienced and seen thus far is as good as it gets! It is not. That is because *"God is Spirit and they that worship Him must worship Him in Spirit and in truth* (John 4:24 KJV)." You have only just begun to know God because He is a Spirit and to truly get to know Him, you have to do so through your spirit.

Your worship should involve your will (your choice to worship Him) and your soul. Your soul is where your emotions reside which demonstrates your attitude toward Him – gratefulness, reverence, love, sorrowful repentance, etc. Your worship should also involve your Spirit. God placed your Spirit inside of you. It knows the mind of God; it knows His will and His heart; it reveals His truth and His word and His ways. You develop each of these areas not by chance but by first desiring more of God, Jesus, and the Holy Spirit.

You and I need the Holy Spirit to come and dwell inside of us after we've been saved. This is called the "baptism of the Holy Spirit". This is a separate experience beyond salvation when the Holy Spirit reveals Christ to you and renews your spirit, which was dead, to life. In the salvation experience, you became "alive" to Christ and dead to sin. You received a new nature that wants to live for Christ. "...*Old things passed away and behold all things became new* (2 Corinthians 5:17)."

Now, when I speak of the "baptism of the Holy Spirit, I am speaking of a mystery that cannot be perceived by our natural senses but is purely supernatural. This is having your empty well inside filled to overflowing and the experience of the Holy Spirit coming to dwell inside of you permanently, and giving you access to His power, anointing, understanding, correction, rebuke, strength, peace, love, and what are called the "gifts of the Spirit". As you "yield to the Holy Spirit" and allow Him to lead and guide you, He empowers you to rule over your soul and emotions and steer them in the right direction as a compass shows us which direction is North, South, East, and West. If you let the Holy Spirit be your compass, He will never, no never steer you wrong!

The Holy Spirit will always exalt the name of Jesus, which is the name above all names. Regarding that highly exalted name of Jesus, Romans 14:11 (NIV) declares, *"It is written:* *"'As surely as I live,' says the Lord, 'every knee will bow before me; every tongue will acknowledge God."*

As you increase your time in prayer and reading the word of God, you will find yourself "naturally" having moments or times where you worship God the Father, Jesus, and the Holy Spirit. God is present with you when you pray. After all, you are communicating with Him, right?

Your prayer is a conversation with Him that is occurring in the here and now. You are not sending text messages, voice mails, or emails up to heaven hoping that, when He gets time, He will get around to reading it or listening to it. Remember, He dwells inside of you if you are born again. You are speaking and communicating to Him "Spirit to Spirit." He's never too busy for you to call on Him, speak to Him, or simply ask a question.

God the father wants to father us and nurture us.

He wants that kind of relationship with you! God the father wants to father us and nurture us. Jesus wants to be our great high priest interceding for us and serving as our example of how to live this life of faith as He did when on the earth. The Holy Spirit wants to be our guide, our teacher, and our demonstrator of the "presence" and "power" of God. The Holy Spirit was sent by Jesus to lead us into all truth and to execute the will of the Father on earth.

Jesus said, *"When that time comes, you won't have to ask me about anything. I tell you for certain that the Father will give you whatever you ask for in my name.* John 16:23 (CEV)." There's one stipulation – we must not ask for the wrong reasons or selfishly to fulfill our own lusts of the flesh, but according to His will. It is the precious Holy Spirit who "acts" on the prayer petitions we make and brings them to pass.

> **The more you commune with the Holy Spirit, the more time you'll want to spend with Him.**

When you come to a place where you know you need "more" of God then you will want to pray more, attend church more, and worship more. You will see an increase in your worship because you can't help to worship Him more as you understand His sacrifice on the cross for you. When you realize all of the precious promises that Jesus has purchased for you, it should cause you to want to get to know this promise keeper. The more you commune with the Holy Spirit, the more time you'll want to spend with Him. "*You will show me the path of life; In Your presence is fullness of joy; In Your right hand there are pleasures forevermore* (Psalm 16:11 AMP)"

Don't settle for only ten percent of God. Go after all of Him that you can possess. You have a lifetime to grow and pursue His infinite wisdom, His love, His fellowship, and His purpose and plan for your life.

Become a pleasing worshiper in whom God delights. After all, that's what we'll be doing in heaven for eternity!

10

A Heart that Chooses Christ Instead of Religion

How do you know if you have a religious Spirit or if you indeed have a God-controlled, God-centered Spirit, which can worship in Spirit and in truth? What is a religious Spirit?

We have already discussed the role that we want the Holy Spirit to play in controlling and strengthening our inner Spirit man so that we operate in the kingdom of God and not the kingdom of darkness. We know that it's the Holy Spirit who equips us to worship and live an overcoming, victorious life in Christ. So how does a religious Spirit or a Spirit of religion differ from the Holy Spirit's guidance in our lives?

John 4:23 (KJV) below explains it:

> *"But the hour cometh, and now is, when the true worshipers shall worship the Father in Spirit and in truth: for the Father seeketh such to worship Him".*

True worshipers worship the Father in Spirit (by the Holy Spirit) and in truth (revelation given by the Holy Spirit). Worshiping the Father by any other revelation or Spirit outside of the Holy Spirit is not true worship.

A Spirit of religion does not emanate from the Father, Jesus, or the Holy Spirit. It is man-made and man created. It is an imitation and counterfeit of true worship and, it lacks the power of true worship. It also doesn't result in fellowship with God. It may look like real worship and it may sound like real worship but, it doesn't yield the results of true worship.

Often, a Spirit of religion brings confusion into the body of Christ and frustration to the person engaging in it. That person may demonstrate devotion with his emotions and actions that are passionate and resolute, however, he remains unchanged in the presence of God. This could go on for many years in a person's life as he wrestles with his flesh and what other people think of them and says about them.

One of the character traits of this type of individual is he desperately wants to be known by everyone for his devotion to God. He seeks recognition for his knowledge of spiritual matters and the works he performs in the body of Christ which he believes points to his spirituality. In addition, this individual seeks acknowledgment for what he does from others, especially those in authority, and he may come into contention with other believers who do not follow the correct behavior, speech, or attitude he believes others should possess. He tends to lack patience or compassion for other believers who have fallen into sin and need prayer and a helping hand to be restored back to the body of Christ. He tends to be critical of those who don't measure up in his eyes to his standards of Christianity.

A Spirit of religion removes the "love" equation from one's Christian walk and places great importance upon outward performance and demonstrations of righteousness. Its focus is on maintaining control at all times of oneself and others in an effort to "appear" righteous while inwardly there are internal conflicts and struggles with one's self-worth. It is a hard taskmaster to those who possess it and unsettling for anyone who comes in conflict with it.

A Spirit of religion does not recognize the meaning of grace as the scripture describes below:

> *Ephesians 2:8-10 (KJV) states, For by grace are ye saved through faith; and that not of yourselves: It is the gift of God: Not of works, lest any man should boast".*

A person under the influence of a religious spirit believes he is the reason for his relationship with the Lord and not that it was a gift of God to *anyone* who will accept it. He believes that because of his good works in the church he is recognized or promoted, and others need or depend upon him. He doesn't understand that all his works are as filthy rags on any given day! God allows us to worship and serve Him despite our shortcomings and missteps. We could never "qualify" ourselves to worship God through our actions or service. In order to please God, we must know that His gift of forgiveness and grace is free to all, and nothing we could ever do could purchase that gift. This is why a person with a spirit of religion doesn't want to see others walk in the grace of God's love and forgiveness. They think they earned what they have received and everyone else must earn it too.

A spirit of religion is cousins to the Spirit of pride. They are close pals. When you operate in a religious spirit, you believe you are the chief reason that you are saved, righteous, holy, and walk upright before God. You believe that you made the right decisions and choices in your life, overcame sin on your own, shunned evil, and so on. This person has little patience or compassion for those he or she sees as weak, or who they believe should have been delivered from their weaknesses and sin by now.

Those among us who are in bondage to this spirit are not bad or insensitive Christians. There may be different reasons why someone may have been put into bondage by satan to this Spirit. So many of our dear saints have endured such shame in their past that they had no control over, nor did they cause. This left scars in their heart and emotions that shaped their thinking and behavior when they first met Christ and accepted Him as Lord. These wounds have not all been addressed even though this believer may have been walking with the Lord for years now. They may still feel a measure of guilt and shame even though they are a child of God. Some of these precious believers have such low self-esteem and this spirit of religion drives them to present a persona that is the opposite of how they feel about themselves. They work so hard at looking the part while inside they are scared, hurting, and they feel naked and bare.

They don't realize that if they would allow the Lord to shine the light on those dark places that all of us have in our lives, He would perform the necessary surgery and circumcise their heart and heal it. Sadly, some have decided that it is too painful to address and to acknowledge it to anyone, including God. However, it doesn't go away and stays there lurking in the shadows. They do not have the peace that Jesus died on the cross for them. They truly love the Lord but, they carry around a secret from their past and/or present that continues to hold them captive. They live in fear of what others think about them or know about their past or present wounds. Daily they feel as if they are carrying around a ball and chain everywhere they go as they exhaust themselves trying to be better at so many things so that others think they are better than how they feel on the inside.

Does having a spirit of religiosity mean you are not saved? Not necessarily. You may very well be saved and love the Lord, however, there are some underlying issues in your heart and in your flesh that were never dealt with after you confessed Christ as your Savior. Although you have obtained salvation through faith in the finished work of Christ, that was only the beginning. For the rest of your life, your flesh (the innermost desires of your heart, both physical and of the mind, will, and emotions) must be renewed daily.

What exactly is "renewing" your mind and how do you accomplish that? I'm glad you asked. To renew your mind is to make it brand new, which implies that you need to replace something that is old or outdated or isn't relevant. You and I, on a daily basis, need to infiltrate our minds with the light of the gospel of Jesus Christ. We need to replace any darkness that resides there with the light of truth in God's holy word – the Bible.

The Bible contains God's thoughts. It is God's message to the world about His plan of salvation for all mankind. It contains the revelation that Jesus Christ is the way, the truth, and the life that we all need. When you understand that you cannot live the Christian life and be spiritually healthy and whole without the Word of God then you will feast regularly upon it.

Reading the word of God alone doesn't automatically renew your mind. The Word must be received or accepted as *the Word of God* by faith. Otherwise, it is just words on a piece of paper that is void of power. Your faith in those words releases the power to change your thinking, which in turn renews your mind.

The Word of God is able to expose the deception in your life and the dark places of sin or error you have been following. It can "wash" away doubt, confusion, and discouragement like water washes a garment clean. When taken daily by faith, it changes your thinking until you begin to think like God and His Word. That is because the Word of God has the backing of heaven. It will not fall to the ground! God is working behind the scenes to reveal His word to us, so we know it is He who has spoken it. He is then making sure that it comes to pass!

> *Isaiah 55:11 (ESV), "So shall my Word be that goes out from my mouth; it shall not return to me empty, but it shall accomplish that which I purpose, and shall succeed in the thing for which I sent it".*

The Word of God is our standard to live by. It helps us to see that, apart from God's transforming power, we have no righteousness of our own. Many believe that studying the Word of God has no purpose or value as long as they believe that Jesus is the Messiah and they say the sinner's prayer of repentance. However, that is just the beginning! There are always areas in your mind and heart that the Lord wants to purify and set free. We are a continual work in progress.

Don't allow pride or the enemy satan to deceive you into thinking that you do not need more of God. He wants to stunt your growth and stop you from receiving your full deliverance. He wants you to accept that counterfeit spirit that tells you that you are okay as you are. He wants to keep you from going through Gods' divine process of purging, cleansing, and deliverance. We all need to walk victorious and to come forth as pure gold.

Take a closer look deep down inside. Are you judgmental of other believers who have not "arrived" so to speak, or do you hurt when you see your sister and brother struggling or when they have fallen into sin? Are you critical of others in ministry that you don't believe measure up or do you pray for them and try to encourage them or help them? Are you the person who always is the one who must point out others' shortfalls and "get them straight" because no one else seems to be able to see what you see? Do you wonder what the ministry or the group you work with would do if you weren't there to fix things or carry out the work? When was the last time your heart truly broke for the people you don't get along with, frustrate you, or make you mad? A tender heart is a characteristic of a believer filled with the Holy Spirit. A believer with a religious (legalistic) spirit struggles to have a tender heart toward others. If this describes you, don't be ashamed or feel condemnation. Ask your heavenly

Father for forgiveness right now and His help to get free. Ask Him to reveal to you the origin of how you were ensnared into this trap of the enemy. He is waiting with open arms just for you!

Also, if you have felt as though there is a glass ceiling above you or around you in the midst of praise and worship and you can't seem to fully break through, ask the Lord to reveal to you what is hindering your worship. We all have times when situations cause us to feel a greater distance from the presence of the Lord. This can certainly happen, however, if you have had many occasions where you know that there is something hindering you from being totally free to worship then ask the Lord to reveal it to you. He wants a closer fellowship with you more than you do. Don't be ashamed or afraid to admit that something is not completely right in your worship experience or, perhaps you simply know that there is more of the Holy Spirit that you need. Don't assume that what you have experienced thus far is all there is! I assure you there is so much more.

Humble yourself now and ask the Lord to change you, to fill you, to forgive you, and to wash you! None of us have arrived at the full measure and stature of Christ (Ephesians 4:13, KJV). We are on a journey! Don't get off the train and set up shop on the first leg of the trip. There are many more stops along the way. There are many more encounters of healing of our soul and deliverance in our flesh as we grow from faith to faith. In addition, there are many more times God will reveal sin in our lives that we must repent of and be freed from by the Holy Spirit. There are also many more inward fillings of the Holy Spirit we have yet to receive. How exciting is that! There are others waiting to be rescued from a life of sin just as we have been rescued. Receive ALL that the Lord has waiting and ready for you!

11

A Heart Healed of Wounds from the Past

One of the traps that satan uses so often against everyone, if he can, is to keep you and me angry at those who have offended or wounded us. From the beginning of creation, he has been lying in wait to manipulate and destroy anyone who would entertain his lies. He deceived Eve in the Garden of Eden but, He didn't stop there. Years later after two sons were born to Adam and Eve, he used an offense to persuade one brother (Cain) to slay His brother (Abel).

In chapter 4 of the book of Genesis, the Bible gives an account of this tragedy in the lives of this family. It explains that, in those days, Cain was a tiller of the ground. In other words, he was a farmer. Abel was a shepherd who kept the herds of sheep. The Bible explains that one day, they both decided to give an offering to the Lord. We really don't know why they chose to do so. We can only assume that, perhaps, the Lord expected to receive an offering from them as a form of worship or thanksgiving. Because God is just, we can be confident in knowing that He would have given instructions on what type of offering they should bring Him. Nevertheless, the scriptures simply tell us that, one day, they both came before the Lord to bring an offering.

Abel brought an offering from the finest firstborn of his flock and the fat also and it was pleasing to God and He accepted it. Cain brought to the Lord an offering from the fruit of the ground but, God did not accept his offering. Cain chose not to follow God's instructions on what an acceptable offering should be.

In Genesis 4:6-7 (NKJV) we have the account of God's response to Cain when he presented His offering:

> *"Why are you so angry?" the Lord asked Cain. "Why do you look so dejected? You will be accepted if you do what is right. But if you refuse to do what is right, then watch out! Sin is crouching at the door, eager to control you. But you must subdue it and be its master."*

In God's own words we see His willingness to accept Cain's offering if he would do what was right. That means he knew that his offering was not what God required *before* he brought it. God also sent a stark warning to Cain that if he refused to do what was right, sin could enter into his heart and soul and it would control him.

The Bible goes on to say that, one day Cain and Abel were in the field together alone. Tragically, Cain decided not to follow God's instructions nor heed His warning. He became angry beyond control. In fact, Cain grew so angry that it drove him to murder his only brother Abel. Abel was an innocent man, guilty of nothing wrong. He simply obeyed God as he was instructed to. It was God who rejected Cain's offering, not Abel.

Why did Cain attack Abel? It was because Cain couldn't lash out at God and take out his anger on Him so, He took it out on his brother instead. Cain wasn't satisfied with going on his way and finding an acceptable offering, bringing it back to God to present so he could receive God's acceptance. No, he wanted to keep Abel from having the honor of God accepting His offering. Envy and hatred filled his heart to the point that he could no longer stand for Abel to live before him. What a sad tragedy for both Cain and Abel and their parents Adam and Eve.

Sin can make us do what we would otherwise consider unthinkable. We sometimes speak about someone being "out of control." This is a perfect example of sin becoming our master and leading us down the wrong path. God said to Cain regarding sin, *"You must subdue it and be its master."*

When offenses come in life and they surely will, as God said, we must be careful not to open the door to sin. Sin is always waiting for the opportunity to enter our hearts. We must subdue it and become a master over it. We have to be aggressive about taking charge of it and not passive.

Remember that satan is the author of sin. He introduced it into the world when he rebelled against God? He wants nothing more than to see our anger fester and grow, just as a wound that doesn't heal can become infected and cause pain. He wants us to constantly feel pain in our souls and in our emotions. He knows if we don't get free of that anger (subdue it as God said), it will open a door of access allowing him to influence our thinking and how we view our lives and others.

Remember that satan is the author of sin.

All he needs is to get our attention when we are most vulnerable, and plant thoughts in our minds that bombard us with reminders of what was said or done to us that wounded us. As we entertain these thoughts, we relive the emotional pain of it. Soon we will begin to recall the events in an even worse light than what actually occurred, which will make us even angrier. If we allow him to plant thoughts into our minds that are not true, he can wound us even deeper than the original offense. If he can get us to meditate over and over on our wounds, he can turn us into victims. Once we identify ourselves as victims instead of victors (children of God who overcome satan Himself and the world), then he can add to our anger a spirit of fear.

If our anger turns to fear, that fear can hold us hostage. Fear can dominate us to the point that we don't reason according to the word of God. It can lead us astray. In fact, our emotions can become so overwhelming that we can lose our perspective on the matter or the people we are involved with. Even facts we know to be true can appear untrue. Circumstances and situations can overwhelm us because our fear is the lens from which we see, hear, and make decisions. Fear is our enemy and satan is the God of fear. He wants a foothold into our wounded soul as a catalyst so he can try to use us to hurt others who have done us no wrong.

Satan cannot read our minds nor can his demons. He can tell, however, if he has no opposition from us because we are not resisting him but, rather entertaining his lies. We are encouraged by scripture to resist the devil as described in James 4:7 (NKJV),

> *Therefore submit to God. Resist the devil and He will flee from you.*

How do you resist the devil? You must submit yourself to God! How do you submit to God? First of all, you must shut down the flurry of thoughts reverberating in your mind. Whether you feel shame, violation, anger, pain, unforgiveness, or you simply want revenge, you have to subdue it. You need to recognize that you need help to move beyond these emotions and that help comes from your heavenly Father when you ask Him. Submit your pain to God. Submit your anger to Him. He already knows where you are in your heart and mind and everything that was done to you or that you may have done. He has to have your permission to intervene and enter into your situation to renew your mind and heal your broken heart. You have to invite Him in and give Him the authority to fix whatever is wrong in your heart and your life. He will absolutely come if you want Him to. Remember that this is what Jesus paid for on the cross – to give you access to the Father. So ask in Jesus' name and the Father will grant the healing and restoration by the Holy Spirit.

> **How do you resist the devil? You must submit yourself to God!**

You can't submit to God to be free from your wounds and, at the same time, submit to satan and walk-in fear, pain, and defeat. You must make a choice. Do you want to keep the hurt because you feel justified in doing so, or do you want freedom? Just remember that the hurt and anger keep you in a prison cell while those who offended you walk around free. You deserve better!

God requires that we forgive whether the offender

deserves it or not because He forgave us of our many sins when we did not deserve it. Seems impossible to do? You can when you submit to God. He will give you the strength to do it. He will give you the power to expel the hate and inhale the love. You will take hold of His promises in His word and KNOW they apply to YOU. You will see His plan for your life unfold right before your eyes and rejoice that He loves you and knows your name.

> **You can't submit to God to be free from your wounds and, at the same time, submit to satan and walk-in fear, pain, and defeat.**

You will grasp the meaning of these scriptures –

> *Oh, give thanks to the Lord, for He is good! For His mercy endures forever. 1 Chronicles 16:34 (NKJV).*

> *He remembered our utter weakness, for His loving-kindness continues forever. And saved us from our foes, for His loving-kindness continues forever. Psalm 136:24-25 (TLB).*

Worship Him and give Him thanks for He has saved you.

12

A Heart that Accepts Jesus' Sacrifice on the Cross for Our Sins

Everyone who has ever been set free from a life of sin, iniquity, and condemnation can testify that the chains of sin and death have been broken over their body, soul, and spirit. They no longer belong to satan and they no longer dwell in His realm of darkness. They no longer have dark thoughts, dark motivations, nor love the darkness His kingdom offers. They are possessors of Jesus' light; they walk in the light; they cultivate the light and they give out the light wherever they go!

There is no condemnation in the light. Condemnation can only exist in the darkness. In the light, there is forgiveness. There are no deceptions or lies in the light; there is only the truth. There is no turmoil or torment in the light; there is only the peace of God. There is no hatred in the light but, unconditional love! Fear cannot exist in the light for fear originates from the fall of Adam in the garden. In the light, there is faith in the Word of God, the love of God, and the power of the cross to set us free and restore us to the Father. We are the children of light because we have become the children of God! Hallelujah!

Let us walk in full assurance that what Jesus Christ did on our behalf is a finished work. In other words, His death, crucifixion, burial, and resurrection have given us authority over every problem, every situation, every failure, every attack, every accusation we will ever face in this life. We have a great high priest who ever lives to make intercession for us (Hebrews 7:25). He has paid the ultimate price for our salvation because He is the ultimate expression of love – how love sees; what love thinks; what love gives; what love does; who love is! Jesus is the manifestation of love!

If you have said the sinner's prayer in the past confessing Jesus Christ as your Lord and Savior but, still find yourself doubting your salvation, then right now is your time to break this doubt and find assurance that your sins have been forgiven.

First of all, do you have doubts that Jesus would forgive you of your sins because in your eyes, they are too horrific, and you don't deserve to be forgiven? Have you ever forgiven yourself for your past or do you still rehearse it from time to time and feel under judgment for it? Do you still carry shame within for what you've done, or do you recognize that you have received the righteousness of God in exchange for your sinful past?

According to Isaiah 64:6 (NLT),

> *"We are all infected and impure with sin. When we display our righteous deeds, they are nothing but filthy rags. Like autumn leaves, we wither and fall, and our sins sweep us away like the wind.*

When we display our righteous deeds, they are nothing but filthy rags. Therefore, our righteousness will never, never be enough to save us. That's why Jesus had to come and live a sinless life so He could be slain as an offering in our place to satisfy the judgment for our sin which was death. The death that you and I deserved for our sin has been paid but, if you don't believe this in your heart and you only believe it in your head, you will continue to expect judgment for your sins. You will never have confidence toward God when you stand in His presence to pray or worship, or to hear His Word preached. Your guilt and the lies from satan will keep you in a place of never being sure if the last time you said the sinner's prayer it worked, and you were heard and forgiven. It will keep you in a place of judging whether God is pleased with you by how much you have done for Him lately. Did you read your Bible enough? Did you pray enough this week? When you think about it, you haven't been to Bible study in a long time. You haven't given as much money as you should to the building fund, etc. You cannot earn your salvation by doing enough in the kingdom of God. There is only one way to salvation as the scripture states below.

Romans 10:9-11 (NIV) says,

> "If you declare with your mouth, "Jesus is Lord," and believe in your heart that God raised Him from the dead, you will be saved. For it is with your heart that you believe and are justified, and it is with your mouth that you profess your faith and are saved. As Scripture says, "Anyone who believes in Him will never be put to shame."

We must all confess with our mouths that Jesus is Lord. Many of us have done this over and over but, the second part is also so crucial – we must *believe* in our heart that God hath raised Him from the dead, and then we shall be saved. WE MUST BELIEVE. We must know beyond a shadow of a doubt that we have salvation because God raised Jesus from the dead and we believe in this fact! We believe that God in the flesh – Jesus – did this just for us. This is not just a

Bible story or some fable – this happened for all mankind; for every generation born and yet to be born. A loving God gave mankind a second chance!

Murder, abortion, incest, rape, stealing, lying, and every sin you can name can't keep you from being forgiven by Jesus Christ. You only have to *repent of your sins* and *confess Jesus as Lord* and *believe in your heart that God raised Jesus from the dead.* God could have decided that certain sins were excluded from salvation and given us a list of what He would forgive and He would not. He knew that no one would be saved if He did such a thing! He could have chosen that only certain people, races, or even genders deserved to be saved. Praise God that, instead, He said this in His Word:

Romans 10:12-13 (NIV) states,

> "For there is no difference between Jew and Gentile—the same Lord is Lord of all and richly blesses all who call on Him, for, "Everyone who calls on the name of the Lord will be saved".

Everyone who calls on the name of the Lord will be saved. That is one of the greatest promises in the Bible! Everyone… everyone… regardless of the sin… who calls on the name of the Lord shall be saved! He says that there is no difference if you are Jewish or non-Jewish (gentile). It also doesn't matter if you are male or female. He is the same Lord over all and He will richly bless all who call on Him! Hallelujah!

If you are ready to belong to Jesus, to submit your entire will to Him and live for Him, then call upon His name. He is going to take your unrighteousness and exchange it for His righteousness so you will have the power to live victoriously over sin. A new life awaits you and the old life of sin will be behind you. You will be "born again" into a new life!

Today, whether you've never received salvation before and forgiveness of your sins or you have been a part of a church body for many years, you can know and settle forever in your heart that you are born again; you are saved.

Begin to thank the Lord and worship Him for what He's done! Just pour out your heart to Him. You can talk to Him about anything. He is listening!

13

Eight Important Reasons to Worship

Worship brings the supernatural from the Spirit realm into our lives! It brings the atmosphere of heaven down here to earth! Worship changes our circumstances here on earth and allows a shift to occur where our present condition and destiny align with the will of heaven! Hallelujah!

Here in this earthly realm are principalities, powers, and spiritual darkness in high places but worship sets up a bunker on the battlefield; it brings in the Calvary in a conflict, it releases all of the firepowers in a firefight; it builds an impenetrable hedge, and builds a wall around us that no power of the enemy can break through or destroy. Worship causes God to arise!!!

Psalm 68:1 (KJV) states:

> *"Let God arise, let His enemies be scattered: let them also that hate Him flee before Him".*

Worship scatters the enemies of God! Worship scatters *our* enemies! Let God arise in our worship and our praise and let His enemies be scattered. Hallelujah!

There are so many reasons to worship God. First and foremost, you can worship your heavenly Father because He not only created you but, made a decision to send Jesus to rescue you from sin and eternal death. You can worship Him for His lovingkindness in choosing to give you life, no matter what the circumstances of your birth were or who your parents are. You can worship God as your Father, your provider, your protector, and your creator. You came out of His very bosom – out of His heart, His mind, and His spirit! You were created in your daddy, Abba Father's, image.

Likewise, you can worship Jesus, the author, and finisher of your faith. He is the author of your faith because it is your faith in His death on the cross, His burial, and His resurrection after three days that is the foundation of your faith. This foundation declares that you are saved, you have eternal life and you are more than an overcomer here in this life! Jesus authored our faith because, without His willingness to take the punishment for our sins and pay the price of death we owed, we would not be reconciled back to the Father. How could we possibly worship the Father if we were never reconciled back to Him? Faith in Jesus as the perfect sacrificial offering is the way back to the Father. The scriptures say that no man can come unto the Father except through Jesus.

Jesus is the finisher of your faith because there is nothing left to be done so that we can have the God kind of faith. You and I have been authorized and deputized to use the name of Jesus to walk in faith and victory here on earth. You have been given authority to use the name of Jesus to defeat the enemy satan in every area of your life. Everything you need to serve God and live holy has already been done when Jesus shed His blood for your salvation. He said on the cross as He hung there suffering, bleeding, and dying, "it is finished" and so it is.

Last but certainly not least, there is much to worship the Holy Spirit for! What a wonderful, beautiful, loving, gentle, and kind God the Holy Spirit is! He is so patient, yet so powerful. He is so Holy, yet so tender. He is so loving, yet His holiness will not allow Him to abide around sin and disobedience. He gently leads and guides us to do what is right in all areas and situations in our lives. He will bring conviction to us of our sins within both our thoughts and actions but, never in a condemning way.

As you worship Him, thank Him for His correction and His rebuke. Give Him thanksgiving and praise because you see His guiding hand over your life. Acknowledge the times He has protected you from dangers seen and unseen. Glorify Him for giving you the power to work and perform in your daily routine. Thank Him for His intervention in your life and in your family to provide favor, protection, provision, and every blessing. Let Him know that you appreciate everything He does for you. Let the Holy Spirit know that you need Him and depend upon Him for His guidance, strength, and peace.

Don't just worship and pray to God the Father, Jesus the Son, and the Holy Spirit only when there is trouble, or you have a need. Let them know, as often as you can, how much you love them, and thank them and appreciate all they have done, and are going to do in your life. Treat them the way you would treat anyone in your life whom you love dearly. Your love, obedience, the sacrifice of praise, adoration, and worship are the greatest things you can offer the "triune" God of the universe who already owns everything and everyone! It's the one thing that God can't give Himself. You have to voluntarily choose to give Him your heart for it will either belong to Him or to satan, the evil one.

I urge you my friend to make the best decision of your life and choose the kingdom of God and draw near to Him and enjoy a lifestyle of worship.

Now, let's take a look at some of the reasons to worship God the Father, Jesus, and the Holy Spirit!

1. *Worship is an act of love between you and God.*
2. *Worship is a form of warfare against the kingdom of darkness.*
3. *Worship allows us to receive the ability of God.*

4. Worship imparts to us the mind of God.
5. Worship bestows upon us the anointing of God with power.
6. Worship enables you to overcome grief and sorrow.
7. Worship breaks the power of demonic bondage.
8. Worship illuminates the soul with the light of the Holy Spirit and the word of God.

14

Worship is An Act of Love Between You and God

Worship is an act of love between you and God. God is love and He wants to give love to us and receive love from us. Yes, God wants to be loved! To love and be loved is the very essence of His nature. That's why, when you are truly in His presence and worshiping Him, one of the first things you will feel is His love. Oh, how it brings such great peace to the soul! It brings an assurance that you belong to Him and He truly cares for you.

Oh, if we only understood how much God longs to be connected in fellowship with us constantly. That was His original plan when He created Adam and Eve. They were in *constant* fellowship spirit to spirit, heart to heart. He felt what they were feeling, and they felt what He was feeling. He loved them so much just as He loves you very much. They are His family. You are also His family if you have been born from above (accepted Christ as your personal Savior). He feels the same way about you as He did about Adam and Eve. You are His special treasure. He wants to be in continuous fellowship with you as well. This is all possible through the blood of Jesus and the Holy Spirit living on the inside of you.

You see, God has been on a quest to recover every lost soul ever born into sin back into fellowship with Him. He hasn't changed His mind about what He intended our lives to be. He still wants to walk in the garden in the cool of the day with His beloved children and talk with them and nurture them and give them dominion over all of His creation. He intended that Adam and Eve, out of their loins, would produce a royal priesthood and a holy nation who would look and behave just like their daddy. Guess what? His will for you is the same – that you would become a royal priest and become a holy citizen of the redeemed ones – the holy nation.

> 1 Peter 2:4-5 (NKJV) states, "Coming to Him as to a living stone, rejected indeed by men, but chosen by God and precious, you also, as living stones, are being built up a spiritual house, a holy priesthood, to offer up spiritual sacrifices acceptable to God through Jesus Christ".

> *1 Peter 2:9-10 (NKJV) states, " But you are a chosen generation, a royal priesthood, a holy nation, His own special people, that you may proclaim the praises of Him who called you out of darkness into His marvelous light; who once were not a people but are now the people of God, who had not obtained mercy but now have obtained mercy".*

What does it mean to be a part of a "chosen generation, a royal priesthood, and a holy nation? Well, to be considered royalty, one must be born into a royal family. As a believer, you were born into the highest royalty that has ever existed, the family of God. What a thought! You are an heir to the wealth and kingdom of your Father God! You are also a joint heir with Jesus Christ who was the first begotten son of God before mankind was created. One of your titles to the throne is that of Priest. You are a kingly priest. What does a kingly priest do? A kingly priest is not only an heir to the fortune of the King but, also one who has access to the King at His throne! That access permits you to make requests or petitions of the throne! Only royal priests can stand before the royal court of heaven and make supplications, prayers, and intercession for others as well as themselves in humble adoration and praise before the King of Kings and the Lord of Lords.

The King holds out His scepter to those who have found favor in His sight. He beckons them to come as citizens of His holy nation. Those who are not holy cannot hold an audience before Him for He *is* holy, and sin cannot abide in His presence. Thanks be to God that the sinless lamb offered for the sins of all those who would receive Him as their Lord and Savior would pay the price to give us access to the King. "God made Him who had no sin to be sin for us so that in Him we might become the righteousness of God" (2 Corinthian 5:21 NIV). Hebrews 4:16 (MSG) explains it further so exquisitely,

> *Now that we know what we have—Jesus, this great High Priest with ready access to God—let's not let it slip through our fingers. We don't have a priest who is out of touch with our reality. He's been through weakness and testing, experienced it all—all but the sin. So let's walk right up to Him and get what He is so ready to give. Take the mercy, accept the help.*

We can never approach the throne of God in our righteousness or good deeds. We can, however, through the righteousness we obtained through the blood of Jesus Christ that has made us holy.

Jesus' sacrifice moved our citizenship from the kingdom of darkness into the holy nation where God's kings and priests reside. As kings, we can decree and command the will of the Father to be done on earth as it is in heaven. As priests, we are given the honor to carry the presence of God as the priests of the old testament days carried the ark of the covenant. Not only does the earth come under the rule and decrees of God whom we represent but, the whole earth is to be filled with the glory of God! When we operate as kings, we carry the authority given by God Himself that we execute on His behalf. Without this authority executed by the righteous, satan would take over the entire earth and destroy everyone made in the image of God – that's every man, woman, boy, and girl.

Proverbs 14:34 (**NKJV**) says, *"Righteousness exalts a nation, but sin is a reproach to any people"*. It is that righteousness that pushes back the forces of evil. Where there is little or no righteousness, wickedness abounds. Where there is no one resisting the forces of darkness, the kingdom of darkness will set up its abode.

You are called to be a royal king and a holy priest to establish the kingdom of God wherever you go and to set up an altar of worship to the King. As you worship, you release a fragrance that fills the atmosphere and it gets God's attention! He beholds the passion and love poured out from your heart toward Him. Your worship is an invitation for Him to come and spend time with you. You are inviting the Ancient of Days, the Everlasting Father, and the Prince of Peace to come and dine with you at a banquet table that *you* have prepared just for Him. No one else in all creation can communicate with you *spirit to spirit and heart to heart.* No one else deserves your worship but Him. And the good news is that He *wants to* accept your invitation. He wants to receive your gift of worship. The Lord delights in it because He delights Himself in *you!*

So now, adorn yourself with your royal garments of praise. Put on your precious jewels of sweet adoration. Present Him with your gifts of thanksgiving and gratefulness. Offer Him your heart and your life forever. After all, isn't your desire to spend eternity with Him! Why wait for an eternity to surrender your all? He can be as near to you now as He will be then. You can have a sweet and glorious fellowship with Him today. He is waiting for your invitation.

Revelation 3:20 (TLB) says:

> *"Look! I have been standing at the door, and I am constantly knocking. If anyone hears me calling Him and opens the door, I will come in and fellowship with Him and He with me".*

Don't make the Lord wait outside of the door of your heart. He is constantly knocking but, you must invite Him in. He will not intrude. He will not barge in. Gently and softly He is calling you. What will your answer be? Well you say, I am not worthy to be in His presence. No one is unless he or she has the covering of the blood of Jesus. Remember, the precious blood of Jesus represents mercy to enter the Holy of Holies for everyone who has received Christ as Lord and Savior.

You can enter boldly because you are royalty. Prepare to come before the Most High God. Begin to worship and watch the holy fragrance oil permeate the atmosphere until the holy one comes in with His glory and splendor! He is more eager to spend time with you than you are with Him. He will take *you* from this glory to even greater glory!

15

Worship is a Form of WARFARE Against the Kingdom of Darkness

Did you know that worship is a weapon of warfare? Yes, it is. It is one of the weapons you have been given since you joined the army of God. Yes, you are in the army of God. You are a soldier. You enlisted when you made Jesus your Lord and Savior. You were not drafted; you signed up voluntarily. And, like all soldiers are expected to fight, you must fight. Why? Because there is an enemy to be defeated. He's not only an enemy of God, *he's your enemy!* You have no choice, but to fight. There are no conscientious objectors allowed in this fight because he will simply destroy them! You can't run away or hide or hope he doesn't notice you because the Bible says this — John 10:10 (NIV) states:

> *"The thief comes only to steal and kill and destroy; I have come that they may have life, and have it to the full".*

Satan is a thief who will do all he can to steal from you, kill you, or destroy you. Jesus has come that you may have life and have it to the fullest!

There is good news. You have been given weapons of warfare that can defeat satan on every side if you use them. They are the sword of the spirit which is the word of God (Ephesians 6:17 NKVJ) that cuts going and coming! You have the name of Jesus that everything and everyone is subject to. *"For the Scriptures say, 'As surely as I live,' says the Lord, 'every knee will bend to me, and every tongue will declare allegiance to God'* (Romans 14:11 NLT)." You have also been given the blood of Jesus that paid the ransom price for your sins so that you now have access to the throne room of heaven. All three of these weapons point to the finished work of Jesus on the cross and it is in your worship that you can exercise all three!

The weapons we fight with are not the weapons of the world. On the contrary, they have divine power to demolish strongholds. 2 Corinthians 10:4 (NIV).

These weapons described have "divine" God-given power that will destroy the strongholds of the devil. You can and should worship in the name of Jesus and bless the name of Jesus. You can speak the word of God as you worship in agreement with what God has declared and revealed in that word. You can declare your right to be cleansed, healed, sanctified, and receive the covenant promises purchased by the blood of Jesus. Humble yourself before the Lord in worship. Humility is so important! Empty yourself before Him and surrender yourself to Him. Let His word wash over you and strengthen you as you read it or meditate on it or speak it. When you need to do warfare, fight in the name that is above every name – Jesus! Declare what is needed shall come to pass in that name. Demons flee at that name. Angels are dispatched because of the authority behind that name.

WORSHIP BELONGS TO THE LORD

Satan and his hosts can't abide where the son of the living God, angelic hosts, and the Holy Spirit are worshiped. Jesus demonstrated this to us when He was tempted by satan after fasting for forty days in the wilderness. One of the three temptations satan presented to Jesus pertained to worship:

> *Then the devil, taking Him up on a high mountain, showed Him all the kingdoms of the world in a moment of time. And the devil said to Him, "All this authority I will give You, and their glory; for this has been delivered to me, and I give it to whomever I wish. Therefore, if You will worship before me, all will be Yours." And Jesus answered and said to Him, "Get behind Me, satan! For it is written, 'You shall worship the Lord your God, and Him only you shall serve.' Luke 4:5-8 (NKJV)."*

Satan can't stand for God to be worshiped (Father, Son, and Holy Spirit). He wants what he will never have – the complete worship of all of mankind and especially of the citizens of heaven! He thought Jesus would want the riches, power, and kingdoms of this world so much that He would be willing to worship him rather than God. He thought that was the reason Jesus came – seeking to sit on the throne of the kingdoms of the earth. He wasn't aware of the true master plan of God to save all mankind through Jesus' death on the cross.

Satan also had a master plan. If he could get Jesus to bow before him then he would have achieved his goal to exalt Himself above God. You see, satan along with one-third of the angels in heaven tried to usurp God's authority and led a revolt in heaven to overthrow the kingdom of God. He failed miserably, praise God, and was cast out of heaven. The account of how satan led a revolt in heaven is recorded in the book of Revelation 12:7-12. When satan tempted Jesus, he thought Jesus would follow him just as one-third of the angels followed him when he rebelled in heaven against the Most High God! Of course, the Bible tells us how Jesus resisted each temptation satan attempted because He understood that worship belongs to God. Jesus knew that we *owe* God our obedience to His word.

Unfortunately, satan is still using that same temptation today and, unfortunately, many have fallen prey to it. Many people throughout the ages have agreed to worship satan in exchange for fame, riches, kingdoms, political positions, witchcraft, drugs, perversion, and many other desires and pleasures. Not all necessarily made a conscious decision to serve satan and reject Jesus. They decided to ignore their conscience and pursue what they knew was wicked, evil, or wrong that led them to become a worshiper of satan – whether they realized it or not.

John 3:8 (**NKJV**) explains this so well,

> *He who sins is of the devil, for the devil has sinned from the beginning. For this purpose the Son of God was manifested, that He might destroy the works of the devil.*

When we live a life of sin, we belong to satan for it was he who introduced sin in the beginning when he rebelled against God. All those who practice sin are just like Him – rebels against the kingdom of God. They don't want to live under the authority of God. They want to establish a different kingdom where they are in authority and don't submit to God in anything. That is the nature of satan and all those who worship Him! However, as the scripture states, the son of God (Jesus) was *manifested that He might destroy the works of the devil* –and so He did! That was why He came. He knew His purpose – to destroy the kingdom of darkness holding many in chains to sin, self-destruction, violence, sickness, suffering, torment, poverty, and rebellion against God.

Once we no longer belong to satan, our worship shifts because our new nature is to worship God alone. We become the children of God and the enemy of *His* enemy which is satan. We engage in warfare in the spirit when we worship the Most High God declaring His word in faith; praying His will into manifestation in the earth; releasing the blood of Jesus in all of its power to break yokes and bondages! We follow the example of our Lord and Savior Jesus when we tell satan to get behind us, for it is written, *I shall worship the Lord my God, and Him only I shall serve.'* satan and His demons have to *shut up and flee* when we rebuke (command or scold) Him.

WORSHIP AND THE POWER OF THE WORD OF GOD

> *And the devil said to Him, "If You are the Son of God, command this stone to become bread." But Jesus answered Him, saying, "It is written, 'Man shall not live by bread alone, but by every word of God.'" Luke 4:3-4 (NKJV).*

In each temptation Jesus faced, He made this statement – "it is written". He could have also said, "it is commanded (by God)". Jesus reminded satan that although he is a fallen angel, he is still subject to the word of God! As satan tempted Jesus to test His deity by turning stone to bread, Jesus did not deny that man needs sustenance to live. He agreed but, He also added that man does not need bread alone. He also needs to live by *every word of God*. Jesus caught satan in a half-truth! Satan neglected to mention that the food of the soul and spirit that man also needs to live is *the word of God*. Satan only talked about the food that the body needs to survive knowing that Jesus was hungry from fasting forty days. Jesus however, understood the full truth. The soul and the spirit will far outlast the body and live in eternity forever – either heaven or hell. The body will live only a short time here on earth in comparison to eternity. The most important food a man needs is *the word of God*!

Jesus is a great example of how to handle satan. When you and I also declare the written word of God, if we have faith in what we are declaring, something manifests because the scriptures are *alive and powerful*. Something will be activated by our faith in the written word of God uttered.

> *Then He brought Him to Jerusalem, set Him on the pinnacle of the temple, and said to Him, "If You are the Son of God, throw Yourself down from here. For it is written: 'He shall give His angels charge over you, To keep you,' and, 'In their hands they shall bear you up, Lest you dash your foot against a stone.' " And Jesus answered and said to Him, "It has been said, 'You shall not tempt the Lord your God.' " Now when the devil had ended every temptation, He departed from Him until an opportune time. (Luke 4:5-9 NKJV).*

Angels will indeed move on assignment to bring to pass what God promises in His word to those who *believe*. In this passage of scripture, once again satan was presenting a half-truth to Jesus. You see, Jesus didn't need to demonstrate anything to satan. Jesus knew who He was – the son of God. It was satan who wanted to see some type of demonstration of His power. It is almost like someone saying to you or me, "I don't believe you are who you say you are. I think you are lying. Show me some proof!" In essence, He dared Jesus. Once again Jesus responded, under the Holy Spirit's direction, by speaking the word of God. He told satan that no one should tempt the Lord *your* God. Yes, satan — do not tempt the God *you* are subject to. Satan was and is no match against the power of heaven behind God's word!

Do you think that satan fled because he was afraid of Jesus? No. He fled because of the power of Jesus' faith in the word of God. Jesus was operating as a man on the earth and not as God. He was subject to the same rules as we are. He had to live by *faith* just as we do. Jesus demonstrated for us how it is done when tempted by satan to sin or fear or walk in unbelief. Use your weapon of the word of God. Worship God with the word. And don't forget, the Holy Spirit is there inside to tell you just what to say as He did Jesus.

Every word we utter or song we sing or prayer we pray that agrees with the power, authority, kingship and the word of God is powerful. It reveals the weakness, defeat, and eternal punishment waiting for satan and the kingdom of darkness. It is a declaration that Jesus alone is King of Kings and Lord of Lords to the glory of God our father.

WORSHIP AND THE POWER OF THE BLOOD OF JESUS

When you need divine protection for yourself or others, "apply" the blood of Jesus. What does it mean to "apply the blood"? When you and I apply the blood of Jesus, we lift up the blood before the enemies of God as a banner that signifies that we are His and we are protected by the armies of the living God. If someone messes with us, they mess with God because we are His children! We have special protection from heaven. We are watched over and ministered to by angelic hosts assigned to us.

Let's take a look at the first example we see in the Bible that points to the blood of Jesus and its power to protect and save. In Exodus 12, Aaron and Moses were instructed by God to prepare the people for the 10th and final plague He was about to release upon the land of Egypt as a judgment against Pharaoh and the Egyptians who would not free the Hebrew people from slavery and oppression. Aaron and Moses directed the Hebrews to take a lamb, without blemish, a male of the first year, and kill it. The blood was to be placed on the top and sides of the doorposts of each family's home. They were also instructed on how to roast and eat the lamb. According to Exodus 12:12-13 (NKJV), God provided a way to protect His people from the judgment coming upon the world (Egypt). Though His people lived among the Egyptians, God was able to protect them.

> 'For I will pass through the land of Egypt on that night, and will strike all the firstborn in the land of Egypt, both man and beast; and against all the gods of Egypt I will execute judgment: I am the Lord. Now the blood shall be a sign for you on the houses where you are. And when I see the blood, I will pass over you; and the plague shall not be on you to destroy you when I strike the land of Egypt.

The blood was applied to the doorposts of their homes so the spirit of death would pass over. It was the only thing that would protect the Hebrews from the same fate as the Egyptians. The lamb that was slain and the blood poured out and applied to their homes pointed to the future death, burial, and resurrection of the Lamb of God, Jesus the Messiah our Lord. If we have accepted Christ as our savior, we are now that *"home"* where Jesus' blood is applied, His blood not only *"saves"* us from judgment, it also protects us from the evil one and cleanses us from all unrighteousness. God told the Hebrews that when He sends judgment and He sees the blood, He will pass over them. It was a *"seal"* of protection identifying who belonged to Him and who did not.

But notice, it was not automatic. The Hebrews had to do something. They had to take action. They had to follow the instructions of the Lord *exactly*. They had to be obedient to seek out exactly the type of lamb they were told to find then take him home and follow every commandment given. They could not choose to ignore God's instructions and expect to live. What if they had chosen a bull instead of a lamb? The destroyer would not have passed over their home. They would have lost their firstborn child just as the Egyptians did.

Being born Hebrew alone didn't qualify them to be saved. Who and where you and I were born also doesn't qualify us to be saved. Being a Catholic, Baptist, Methodist, Presbyterian, Pentecostal, or belonging to any other religious group also doesn't qualify us. Even believing there is a God or supreme being doesn't. You see even today, God has given us a detailed set of instructions to follow to be saved from the judgment to come.

Just as the last plague of judgment came upon the Egyptians on that day, there is an eternal judgment coming that He wants us to escape. That is an eternity of damnation spent in Hell. You can escape that future judgment if you accept that Jesus died for your sins and you want to live a new life with Jesus as Lord. When you make that decision, it is as if you have sought a lamb (Jesus) without blemish and brought that lamb into your home (your spirit, soul, and body) as the Hebrews did.

Now, let the "word of your testimony" be that you boldly proclaim your faith in the blood of Jesus and your right to use it. So worship Jesus being ever so thankful for the blood and its power. Sings songs of deliverance because of the blood of the Lamb and the word of our testimony and that we loved not our lives not even unto the death.

WORSHIP AND THE NAME THAT IS ABOVE EVERY NAME

> *Therefore God also has highly exalted Him and given Him the name which is above every name, that at the name of Jesus every knee should bow, of those in heaven, and of those on earth, and of those under the earth, and that every tongue should confess that Jesus Christ is Lord, to the glory of God the Father. Philippians 2:5-11 (NKJV).*

God, by His divine providence, wisdom, and love has placed everything that exists under the authority of the name of Jesus. To put it another way, there is no one in heaven, or on the earth, nor in hell beneath the earth… no not anyone… who will not be subject to *Jesus and His majestic name*. Everyone will bow their knee before Him – either in this earthly realm or in the future dispensation to come. Everyone, who was ever created, even His enemies, will bow before Him and confess that He is Lord.

Before you and I were created, and long after we have gone to the grave, the name of Jesus will still be worshiped, taught, preached, and sung throughout generations. God the Father chose this special name for His earthly son before He was even born. In Matthew 1:20, God gave the following instructions to Joseph who was engaged to Mary, the mother of Jesus, on exactly what to name His son when He was born:

> *But while He thought about these things, behold, an angel of the Lord appeared to Him in a dream, saying, "Joseph, son of David, do not be afraid to take to you Mary your wife, for that which is conceived in her is of the Holy Spirit. And she will bring forth a Son, and you shall call His name Jesus, for He will save His people from their sins."*

The name "Jesus" was chosen purposefully so it would speak to the mission and destiny of Jesus *"for He will save His people from their sins."* Every time that name is spoken, we declare His earthly mission to save mankind.

> *For the Scripture says, "Whoever believes on Him will not be put to shame." For there is no distinction between Jew and Greek, for the same Lord over all is rich to all who call upon Him. For "whoever calls on the name of the Lord shall be saved." Romans 10:11-12 (NKJV).*

Anyone, everyone who calls on the name of Jesus, no matter what his or her condition is, *shall be saved!* The name of Jesus is the *key* that unlocks the door to eternal life. You see, in that name we have victory. We no longer have to be a slave to sin. When our earthly life ends, we can look forward to eternal life with Jesus and not an eternity in hell with satan and his demons. We cannot enter heaven through any other means but through that name. Nothing else will qualify us for entrance in heaven except being washed in the blood of the lamb, through repentance of our sins, and believing in that wonderful name.

For a little while longer, it may be months or years, we have been given a *choice* as to whether we will worship and submit to that name. But, there is coming a day when God the Father will judge the living and the dead and He will set up the throne He has promised His son Jesus. He will reign in majesty and splendor for all the world to see. Every demonic force will be crushed and put in subjection to Him. Jesus will reign over all the earth as King of Kings and Lord of Lords!

God the Father has declared that throughout eternity His name is to be worshiped and honored. We have the awesome opportunity and privilege to worship Him now, here on earth. We *willingly* bow our knees before our king. We gratefully acknowledge His deity and His wisdom and might. We lovingly bestow upon Him our thanksgiving for His sacrifice as noted in Hebrews 12:2 (NKJV),

> *Looking unto Jesus, the author and finisher of our faith, who for the joy that was set before Him endured the cross, despising the shame, and has sat down at the right hand of the throne of God.*

The name of Jesus has not only provided us the means to be saved and belong to the family of God, but it is also our means to defeat the powers of darkness in our everyday lives. You know, God chooses not to take us instantly to heaven once we are saved. No, we must continue to live out our lives here in this earthly realm where others still don't know Him. He wants us to remain as witnesses and light in that darkness so they can find salvation just as we have. We are to share the good news of the gospel of Jesus Christ with others and to demonstrate *His power* on the earth! One of the ways we can do that is through the power that is in the name of Jesus. Jesus explains below that He has given us permission to ask the Father for what we need in His name:

> *You did not choose Me, but I chose you and appointed you that you should go and bear fruit, and that your fruit should remain, that whatever you ask the Father in My name He may give you. John 15:16 (NKJV).*

Jesus said, *"whatever you ask"*. He didn't specify to only ask for food and raiment and a place to sleep. He didn't restrict what you could ask for by naming specific things. What if the God of the universe stood before you and asked you to look around at His creation and tell Him what you wanted, what would you say? Would you choose to be the wealthiest person alive? Would you choose to be healthy for all of your days? Would you choose to own businesses or be famous throughout the world? How about making some type of lasting social change in the world? What would be the most valuable thing you could possess in this life? I submit to you that the most valuable thing on this earth is a man's or woman's, soul.

Souls are the most valuable thing to God the Father, Jesus the Son, and the Holy Spirit. If you choose earthly treasures and pursuits, they won't last more than one hundred and twenty years that man has been appointed to live on this earth. Your soul, however, is eternal. The greatest thing we can ask the Father, in Jesus' name, is to see the kingdom of darkness defeated in our lives, our family, friends, neighbors, strangers, and all those held captive. Use the name of Jesus to set the captives free! Declare their freedom from sickness, poverty, wickedness, perversion, suicide, destructive sins (alcoholism, drug abuse, etc.), hopelessness, abandonment, rejection, depression, depravity, sexual sins, and death. The angelic hosts are waiting for us to use that name so they can spring into action to do the kingdom of darkness harm and rescue the hurting.

Yes, we do need natural things but, they will eventually perish. Our souls never will. We want to spend eternity with Jesus and the saints who have gone on before us. We want to take as many as we can who receive Jesus through our witness during our lifetime. This is the fulfillment of Jesus' commandment to every believer to win the lost. We get our strength and renewal to do so by spending time in worship with the Father, the Son, and the Holy Spirit. If we have a willing and obedient heart then we will be guided by the Holy Spirit where to go and with whom to share the good news that others shared with us. We will not be fearful for, as Revelation 12:11 states, "*...they loved not their lives unto the death.*"

Now that we have tasted victory through Christ Jesus, we won't turn back to our old way of living and thinking. The past is behind us and laid at the foot of the cross. The future is yet to be written but –

> *Being confident of this very thing, that He who has begun a good work in you will complete it until the day of Jesus Christ; Philippians 1:6 (NKJV).*

Praise God forevermore!

16

Worship Allows Us to Receive the Ability of God

We could not worship the Lord if we had not already received the ability to do so from God. How can this mortal, sinful flesh know how to worship God or even desire to do so? It's because, once we were born again, we received the Holy Spirit who renewed our mind and Spirit and reconnected us to the Father through the Son Jesus Christ. We were once dead in our sins but, salvation through faith in Jesus Christ resurrected our Spirit to communion and fellowship with God. The Holy Spirit not only resurrected our spirit, but He also revealed to us who we are in Christ Jesus. He reveals that our inheritance in God has given us the keys to the kingdom!

> *Matthew 16:19 (AMP) states, "I will give you the keys (authority) of the kingdom of heaven; and whatever you bind [forbid, declare to be improper and unlawful] on earth will have [already] been bound in heaven, and whatever you loose [permit, declare lawful] on earth will have [already] been loosed in heaven".*

Jesus has handed us the keys to the Kingdom of heaven! In other words, He gave us the authority of heaven. That means we can do exactly what He can do. Can you fathom that?

Just think, if you were a teenager and you just got your driver's license but, you had no access to a car then all the driver's license could do for you is provide identification. However, if someone such as your father trusted you to drive his car, he would hand you the keys and let you go for it. With his keys, you could open the car the same as he could. You could turn the key in the ignition and start the car as he could. You could put it in drive and go wherever you need to as he could. When he handed you the keys, he authorized you to use the vehicle. Guess what? We have been given the ability of God to forbid on earth what's forbidden in heaven and to permit on earth what is permitted in heaven.

If sickness is not permitted in heaven (and it's not!) and we bind it on earth, the sickness must flee in the name of Jesus. If demons are not allowed in heaven (and they are not!) and we bind them on earth, then they must obey us and flee as they would obey Jesus. If the needs of everyone in heaven are met (and they are) and we loose that on earth then the angels will go forth to bring that prosperity to pass here on the earth.

Here's another promise in the word of God that we have been given power over the demonic realm, over sickness, and disease through the name of Jesus:

> Mark 16:17-18 (NIV) says, "And these signs will accompany those who believe: In my name they will drive out demons; they will speak in new tongues; they will pick up snakes with their hands; and when they drink deadly poison, it will not hurt them at all; they will place their hands on sick people, and they will get well."

What good would it be to carry around the keys to the kingdom in your pocket after being given all that ability and authority from God, and never use them to do anything? If you don't know you have been given the keys, it's easy to do that. If you don't believe by faith that it's possible for you to get the same results as Jesus, you might not use them. Maybe you simply don't want to be used by God to minister to others' needs and to set the captives free. Whatever the issue is, something must ignite your faith to use the authority every believer has been given.

Worship is one of the ways you can come into agreement with the word of God and activate the ability of God. Worship puts us in a special atmosphere where our faith is especially heightened. You enter the realm of the glory – the manifested presence of God. You will become aware that nothing is impossible for God. God even uses ordinary people like us to break bondages, chains, and strongholds off ourselves and others. As the Lord communicates His will for our lives, we can step out in faith and declare with authority and power that by His stripes we were healed. We can command every hold of the enemy to be broken in Jesus' name. We can loose (declare) blessings to come and command lack to go. The very presence of God, as we worship in the glory, speaks to our Spirit to trust Him to decree a thing with authority and to break all the power of the enemy. Worship turns our attention to the Lord, and we are caught up, swept up in His love and divine favor toward us. As a loving Father, He will remind us to not fear anything or anyone and to put our trust wholeheartedly in Him because He cares for us.

As we worship, the Lord may speak a word to our hearts. He may bring a scripture we've heard before to our remembrance. He may minister to us through the song that is being sung at the time or through the prayers we offer up to Him. His ultimate desire is that we take back the ground the devil has stolen from us and that we execute God's authority in the earth as His sons and daughters. He wants us to use the keys of the kingdom and to demonstrate the ability of God in us. Let's take hold of this as truth.

Please repeat this declaration of faith that the ability of God will operate richly in your life:

> *God is My Father. Jesus is my Lord and Savior. The Holy Spirit is my helper and MY guide. My heavenly Father has commissioned me, as a born-again believer to operate on His behalf in the earth and to carry out His will in the earth. My Lord and Savior Jesus died on the cross to take back the keys (authority) from the devil. Jesus defeated the devil and made a spectacle of Him openly and He has given me the keys to the Kingdom. The Holy Spirit's assignment is to reveal Jesus, carry out the will of the Father, release that power to every believer, and fulfill God's promises in the covenant He made with Abraham on the earth. As I yield to the Holy Spirit, He will come in, dwell in me, and abide with me. He will make my heart His home. He will purify me, cleanse me, strengthen me, and give to me the ability of God!*

17

Worship Imparts to Us the Mind of God

The more I have yielded to the Holy Spirit over the course of my life, the more I have become aware of how much and how often I don't have the mind of God on most matters. The Holy Spirit will gladly come into any part of your mind, body, and soul that you give Him access to. You must decide to open the door to your world and let Him come in. Once He does, you must decide if He can remain there or if He's just a visitor you will soon ask to leave.

For instance, you can decide if He can only come into your presence on Sunday mornings when you are at church but, when you leave He must depart. After all, there are so many responsibilities you have and so many expectations people have of you. If only your life were different, you could make more time for Him, right? Somehow though, when a crisis confronts us, we do find a way to call on the name of the Lord for answers and help. He quickly shoots from the last place in our priorities to the first place in a hurry. We can make time for Him when we are in trouble, we need answers to our problems, and we need financial help. We definitely have time for Him when we need healing and our minds are in distress. It is easy to see that we cannot handle those things but, there is a God in heaven who can. We are not always sure if He will hear us and answer our prayer, especially when we know we haven't been serving Him and honoring Him as we should. Still, we hope the Lord will hear us when we ask for His help.

We want to hear His voice. He is now welcome to influence our thinking and our thought life because we don't know what to do. What we have tried is obviously not working. What we need is the mind of Christ on the matter. We don't know what will happen in the future but, we know He does. We may not have the resources needed in the situation we are facing but, He does.

We may be looking at prison time, lawsuits, penalties, or fines because we have done something wrong or we are being falsely accused. We need an audience with God to ask what happened and why it happened. We need to know what the Lord wants us to do about it even if it's the very thing we don't want to do. We need the strength to humble ourselves before God and accept His will.

The Holy Spirit will reveal all these things to us if we ask Him. He will give us the mind of God when we make time for the Lord in our lives. That's why we suddenly turn to God when trouble strikes. Internally, we know that we MUST make time for God because we need His help. Well, how about making time for Him all of the time and avoiding many of the problems in the first place! If we make time for Him every day then we have access to His mind on all matters! Doesn't that make so much more sense than waiting until trials come and troubles arise to find out what God wants us to do to fix it? Yes, it does!

Every day we can know the mind of God through the study of His holy Word, through spending time in prayer with Him, and through worshiping Him. Every day, you and I have the opportunity to worship the Lord. It is truly an opportunity we should not take lightly. Today will only last 24 hours and then it becomes a part of history never to be repeated or relived. When it's over, every opportunity that was available in this present day is gone. Today, you can ignore the Lord of glory and not invite Him into any of your decisions, thoughts, or actions. He can either be relevant or irrelevant to what takes place in your world today. The choice is yours.

If you have been so blessed as to know that you need Him in every part of your day and your life, I encourage you to not only read His word daily but pray to Him about everything and worship Him. However, you don't have to stop throughout the day and go to the synagogue or a church building to do this. Your physical location doesn't matter. You can set up a spiritual altar wherever you are! Remember that the Holy Spirit lives inside of you if you are a born-again believer. God is with you wherever you are now! If you are a truck driver by profession, you can keep the Word of God in that truck, or pull it up on your computer device or phone and read it when you get a chance and meditate on it throughout the day. If you work in an office and you typically have a busy day, you don't have to stop and go to a quiet room or your car to pray. You can meditate on the word of God and whisper prayers to the Lord throughout the day. You can also speak them in your thoughts if you can't say them out loud. He hears you just the same. You can whisper a prayer for a co-worker, or for success with a project you have been assigned. You can pray a simple prayer such as "thank you for helping me with my work today. You may know of someone who is facing difficult circumstances in their lives and you can pray a short prayer for them.

You can also worship the Lord throughout the day. Maybe all you can say during the day is "I love you Lord" or, "I worship you Lord and I bless your holy name" as you think about Him. That is a form of worship. It is not necessary to have music around, nor a choir, musicians, or a praise team. The worship you offer to God is from within your heart and it is an expression of your thoughts toward Him. It's your generous love poured out to Him because He first loved you.

You can worship the Lord driving in the car or while you are shopping. You can worship Him while you are washing the dishes or doing chores. All it takes is turning your heart and your mind toward Him and having a desire to speak to Him and give Him your love and adoration. The more you worship the Lord and you really want to involve Him in your daily living, the more the Holy Spirit will speak to your heart and mind to reveal what the mind of God is about your circumstances and what the will of God is for your life. If you are also studying the Bible, He will also bring scriptures to your remembrance and help you to understand them better and how they apply to your life.

This scripture confirms this truth:

> *John 14:26 (KJV), "But the Comforter, which is the Holy Spirit, whom the Father will send in my name, He shall teach you all things, and bring all things to your remembrance, whatsoever I have said unto you".*

The Holy Spirit is such a wonderful teacher and friend. He would not be either of these if He didn't also correct us when we sin and rebuke us when our mind, thoughts, and will do not line up with the mind of Christ. He wants to bring as much of the light of God, the mind of God, and the will of God into our world as we allow Him to. It is our choice.

18

Worship Bestows Upon Us the Anointing of God with Power

To fulfill the call of God upon our lives, we must have the anointing of God. What is the "anointing" of God? It is duanamis power that is interpreted as the power of God. Duanamis (pronounced doo'-nam-is) is a Greek word defined as miraculous power, strength, might, ability (Strong's Concordance #1411). It is a power that we do not naturally possess but, must be given to us by God. It does not emanate from our physical, mental, or intellectual prowess. This power belongs to God and, at His will, is given to men and women who will carry out His will on the earth.

Every day men and women attempt to carry out God's work and will without the anointing of God. They will try to apply natural solutions to spiritual problems. They will attempt to use human reason to complete the assignments given to them by the Lord. However, God doesn't operate at the lower level of mere men. Men and women must rise up to the level of God.

Isaiah 55:9 (KJV) expresses it this way,

> *For as the heavens are higher than the earth, so are my ways higher than your ways, and my thoughts than your thoughts.*

We need the anointing of God because we simply don't think or act like God would have us to without it!

Let's take a look at an example of duanamis power in the following scriptures that transformed ordinary men into world shakers:

> Matthew 10:11 (KJV) states, "And when He had called unto Him His twelve disciples, He gave them power against unclean spirits, to cast them out, and to heal all manner of sickness and all manner of disease".
>
> Matthew 10:7-8 (KJV) says, "And as ye go, preach, saying, the kingdom of heaven is at hand. Heal the sick, cleanse the lepers, raise the dead, cast out devils: freely ye have received, freely give".

Here we see that Jesus called His twelve disciples to Him as He prepared to ascend back to heaven. His work on earth, as the lamb of God sacrificed for the sins of all, was finished. As the disciples came to Him, Jesus gave them power over all unclean spirits so that they could cast them out. The power they received over unclean spirits also meant they were given power over the Kingdom of darkness itself. He gave them the power to rule and reign over the kingdom of darkness and to take its territory back for the kingdom of God. Wherever the kingdom of darkness was ruling in the lives of people, the disciples received power to overtake those evil powers and to kick them out! How could Jesus give the disciples this power? It was because He had been anointed by God the Father as the following scripture describes:

> *Acts 10:38 (KJV) states, "How God anointed Jesus of Nazareth with the Holy Spirit and with power: who went about doing good, and healing all that were oppressed of the devil; for God was with Him".*

Jesus gave the disciples exactly the same Holy Spirit and power He had received from God the Father. He commissioned them to demonstrate the same ministry He had done. Think of that. They had the right to perform the same miracles as Jesus and they possessed the anointing to carry it out.

The next part of Matthew 10:11 says that Jesus gave the disciples the power to "heal all manner of diseases," which means every disease that has ever existed or is yet to exist! Hallelujah! They were given *all* power over *all* diseases.

The last verse adds another dimension of power given to the disciples by Jesus – the power to raise the dead! Jesus could give this power to the disciples because He received all power over hell and death when He was crucified. He went to hell and took the keys of death and hell from satan and afterward was resurrected. Jesus paid the price for all mankind as the perfect sacrifice for all sin. Death could not keep Him in the grave. Hell could not hold Him, prisoner, either! He descended to hell because He bore all the sins that you and I had committed. Because He lived a sinless life, satan didn't realize Jesus was qualified to regain the authority satan obtained when He tricked Adam and Eve in the Garden of Eden. Jesus beat satan at His own game! As a matter of fact, the Bible declares this about that defeat,

> *"He canceled the record of the charges against us and took it away by nailing it to the cross. In this way, He disarmed the spiritual rulers and authorities. He shamed them publicly*

by His victory over them on the cross." (Colossians 2:14-15 NLT)

Once Jesus paid the price with His life, He then had the right to regain the authority that God had given Adam when He created Him. Adam was given all authority over the earth after God created him. He reigned over the earth with his wife Eve until the day they sinned. God gave them access to everything He created on the earth except one tree. This was the Tree of the Knowledge of Good and Evil. God warned them to never eat of that tree. One day satan entered the Garden of Eden, where they dwelled and tricked Eve into eating from the tree. Adam looked on as this encounter took place and after Eve ate, he chose to eat also. That one act of disobedience plunged the earth and all of mankind into darkness. Adam lost his God-given authority over the earth and turned it over to satan that day but, praise God Jesus regained it and gives that authority and power to whomsoever He wills.

Thus, as previously quoted in Matthew 10:1, Jesus is giving that same power to the disciples. The disciples now have the keys to death and hell meaning they have the power to raise the dead. Notice that Jesus told the disciples to go and preach; that is, go and tell others that the kingdom of God has come. What kingdom? It is the kingdom restored to man because Jesus purchased it with His own blood.

When we believe we too have been anointed to do what Jesus did here on the earth then we also believe that we have authority (given by Jesus) and we have power (through the Holy Spirit). This anointing was not just for Jesus and the disciples. It is for you today! When we obey God as the disciples did and go and tell others that there is hope for sickness, depression, and any bondage from satan, that is an act of worship for our King Jesus. We are submitting our hearts and will to serve the victorious one who is forever seated on the throne. He has ransomed every generation from eternal death. Worship is not just words of adoration or gestures of praise and honor for our Lord Jesus. Worship is also aligning our will with God the Father's will. It is also heeding the promptings of the Holy Spirit as He directs us in exactly how to carry out the Father's will.

An atmosphere of worship is conducive to activating the anointing of God! We are waiting, ready, and willing to receive whatever God wants to release in our lives. As we worship, we desire more of God and more of the kingdom of God. We want the will of God and the Holy Spirit is ready to release it to us. We need the anointing of God to do the will of God. Let's worship and believe by faith that God is anointing us afresh each time we worship and enter His presence! Let's change the way we see our worship time with the Lord. It's activation time! It's another opportunity to be empowered with a fresh anointing from God to handle whatever awaits us that day; that week; that month; that year; and the rest of our lives. We want God's anointing not just for ourselves but, also because Jesus desires to see us walk in His footsteps and to do His exploits!

19

Worship Enables You to Overcome Grief and Sorrow

There was a time in my life when my husband and I endured great sorrow after the death of our baby son. He was only three and a half weeks old. He was born with Down's Syndrome and we knew four and a half months into my pregnancy that he would be born with it.

As is routinely done now, I had an amniocentesis procedure, and an ultrasound performed around twenty weeks into the pregnancy to check for abnormalities. This revealed the condition. The news was shocking and very difficult to hear. What made this even more difficult was how the news was relayed to me by the Radiologist who reviewed the results of the ultrasound. He explained the diagnosis and briefly what possible complications could occur during the pregnancy as well as to our baby. Subsequently, he explained to me that I could abort the pregnancy. I was so shocked and numb that I did not even respond.

Once my husband and I had time to process it all, our wonderful born-again OB/GYN called us into his office to meet with Him. He wanted to talk to us and find out what we wanted to do going forward. We decided to have one more amniocentesis procedure believing by faith that it would show that maybe the first procedure wasn't accurate or that our baby was miraculously healed and would be normal.

The second procedure was scheduled just a few weeks after the first. This time, I waited anxiously for the results in the examination room as I continued to pray. Finally, the doctor entered the room to give me the results. To my surprise, it was the same Radiologist who performed the test the first time. As he gave me the same diagnosis of Down's Syndrome, he immediately began to scold me and ask "Didn't you understand the last time that you needed to abort the pregnancy?" He was actually disturbed that I had not had an abortion but, instead was having a second amniocentesis procedure. His words cut through me like a knife as if I wasn't already bleeding inside from heartbreak and fear. He saw our child not as a human being but as a "problem" that needed "fixing" through an abortion. I shudder to think of all of the mothers he encouraged to do the same.

Well, we never considered killing our baby. Our son was born full-term and we were so happy to have him but also understandably worried. His heart was severely deformed.

Not only did it not have four chambers, it in no way resembled the normal formation of a heart. He also had some of the other traits characteristic of a child with Down's Syndrome.

In his short life, He spent time in three hospitals. He was born in the first hospital and discharged after two weeks. We were only able to have Him home for a few days before he started to have complications and was taken to the emergency room of a second hospital. They informed us they were not equipped to care for Him due to his medical condition. We were told that he might have a chance of survival if we allowed him to undergo open-heart surgery. There were only three hospitals on the East Coast equipped to perform that specific surgery. We decided that if it could save him then we wanted to try.

As soon as possible, he was transferred to a third hospital where he underwent the surgery. Sadly, he didn't survive it and we were so devastated and hurt. I began to ask God, "Why?" "How could this keep happening to us!"

You see, we were blessed with two beautiful children who were healthy and strong but, in the past, we had lost another child. After our 1st child was born, we went through another difficult pregnancy, which resulted in our baby boy dying in utero in the sixth month. During that pregnancy, I was also diagnosed with pre-eclampsia and hospitalized for nearly one month. While in the hospital, I progressively got worse with severe pre-eclampsia and was diagnosed with kidney failure. Once again, I was encouraged to have an abortion by the hospital nephrologist, the cardiologist, and the maternal-fetal specialist so my kidneys could be biopsied and treated. Also, once again our born-again OB/GYN let us know that he disagreed with the abortion, but he wanted to make sure that we received each specialist medical opinion.

Abortion was never an option for us. We prayed; our friends prayed; our church prayed, and our families prayed. Sadly, our son did not survive and I left the hospital with kidney failure, grief, and an uncertain future. An amazing thing began to happen over the course of the next year. Month by month, test after test, my kidneys were healing! One year after I delivered our son, my kidneys were normal! They are still normal to this day, praise God! Another miracle took place after that season. I delivered a healthy, full-term baby girl two years after my kidney failure diagnosis! Our baby did not receive His miracle but, by the grace of God, I did.

The death of our first son was very difficult for sure. The death of our last child was even more devastating because I was not just full of grief and sorrow, I was angry. I somehow descended to a place and mindset where I was angry at God. I complained to the Lord that something was grossly wrong about burying another child. How could that be? Why didn't He do something? I remember in my grief and anger saying to Him, "Look at all of the people abusing children and aborting them Lord. Some even abandon them but, we want children. We want to love and care for them". It was a low time in my life – a really low time. I questioned God's love for us and measured it by the trials and tribulations we faced. I held God responsible for what He had nothing to do with! He didn't cause Down's Syndrome in our son. He didn't cause my body to develop pre-eclampsia or kidney failure. God takes the rap for so many things that go wrong in this world and in our lives. Yet, His stubborn love still pursues us with arms open wide waiting for us to call Him "Daddy", "Father", "Lord", "My Healer", "My Peace", "My Deliver". Our fallen nature searches for someone to blame when bad things happen. Too many times, we falsely accuse God.

One of the amazing things I experienced during this time was that the Holy Spirit never abandoned me though I was offended. He never left me alone. He never cast me off. He continued to love me in my anger. How can I say that? It is because, when I would cry and grieve privately, His still small voice; His presence would tell me to worship. I can't explain it. It didn't make sense to me because the LAST thing I wanted to do was worship. I didn't feel like worshiping. In fact, sometimes I was crying so uncontrollably that I felt that I would never be over it. Nevertheless, the Holy Spirit would gently move upon me to worship. So, I did.

I would sing worship songs while crying at the same time. I would sing and cry and I would feel strength from on high each and every time. I can't explain it but, it is true. I would eventually regain my composure and move on with whatever I needed to do at that time. Also, I noticed that over time, my grieving sessions were becoming less frequent and I was feeling stronger and stronger day by day. During those times of worship, as I was grieving, I felt as if soothing warm oil was being poured over my soul. I believe that as I worshiped, God was performing surgery on my broken heart, which felt as if it was broken beyond repair. He alone was able to put it back together again, hallelujah!

I also eventually came to repentance and asked for forgiveness for falsely accusing the Lord. Though I sought answers asking the Lord many times, "Why Lord did this happen to us – not once but twice?", I never got an answer. I reached the point where I didn't even need an answer. I remember telling the Lord that, even though I didn't understand it all, I could never deny that He loved us even though I questioned it based on what happened. What happened to my family and I had nothing to do with His love for us. What more could He do to show us His love than dying on the cross for us? I asked the Lord for His forgiveness and I received it and I did not walk in condemnation. I thanked Him for His compassion, mercy, and long-suffering with me and I received His fresh revelation through the following scripture: Psalm 34:19 (KJV) states,

> "Many are the afflictions of the righteous: but the Lord delivereth Him out of them all".

In this life, afflictions come – even to the righteous. Grief and sorrow will come at some point to everyone – even followers of Jesus but, the Lord – Jehovah, Adonai, El Shaddai – delivers us from them all! Hallelujah! He will be there with us. He will take us through it to the other side. We will overcome every trial, affliction, and obstacle because Jesus has overcome the world!

Listen to how John 16:33 (KJV) states it,

> "These things I have spoken unto you, that in me ye might have peace. In the world ye shall have tribulation: but be of good cheer; I have overcome the world".

If your heart is broken today or heavy-laden, do the opposite of what your soul wants you to do, which is to become discouraged or depressed, or angry. Put your hope in the Lord. Psalm 42:5 (AMP) states,

> "Why are you in despair, O my soul? And why have you become restless and disturbed within me? Hope in God and wait Expectantly for Him, for I shall again praise Him for the help of His presence."

Again I say, put your hope in the Lord. Expect Him to do something about your plight. Wait expectantly. That means waiting on God expecting Him to move. Turn your heart toward the Lord and not your sorrow or your fears. Worship the Lord. Thank Him for being your help and your strength.

If you need forgiveness, then ask for it with a sincere heart that wants to turn around and live the right way and go in the right direction. Thank the Lord for His mercy and grace in your life that Jesus purchased by His death on the cross. Thank Him for His power being released in your life to overcome sickness, disease, poverty, lack, and all the power of the enemy against you! Give Him praise and honor. Thank Him for dying on the cross for your sins. Thank Him for the blood of Jesus. Yes, the blood of Jesus! For there is power in the blood. Worship Him as King of Kings and Lord of Lords. Sing to Him; dance before Him; lift up your hands and praise Him; pour out your heart to Him. Then you will feel your strength renewing as the hand of the Lord comes upon you.

You may not "feel" like praising Him or worshiping Him. You may feel so weak that you can hardly mutter a word. By faith, if you give Him whatever you have to offer Him right now, He will take notice and come and strengthen you just as He has promised in His Word. *"...he will never leave you nor forsake you* (Hebrews 13:5 NKJV). Your heart will become lighter because you shall take His yoke upon you. Matthew 11:30 (AMP) says it like this, *"For My yoke is easy [to bear] and My burden is light."*

Your life shall truly change as you learn to worship through any circumstance, trial, or tribulation. Remember, your worship is a sacrifice and offering to the Lord. It is precious to Him because you must exercise your faith to worship Him during trials. You must choose your faith in His love for you over the pain, disappointment, and maybe even anger that you feel. As you make that sacrifice to bless Him and enter His presence, His healing balm will be applied to your heart.

Jesus is the only one who can bring healing to your broken heart and wipe away every tear. Your very tears can become worship if you are pouring out your heart to the master and letting Him know that through your pain, you are holding on tight to Him and asking Him to be your Father. You may feel that you will never stop crying and hurting. It may feel as though someone has placed a hole in your soul and that nothing will ever fill it. No matter how much it hurts right now, even if all you can do is just cry, just know that He knows what is in your heart. He sees every question you have, and He will walk this journey of healing with you as long as you need Him to. Don't give up!

> *"Live under the protection of God Most High and stay in the shadow of God All-Powerful. Then you will say to the Lord, "You are my fortress, my place of safety; you are my God, and I trust you" (Psalm 91:1-2 CEV).*

"You are my hiding place; You, Lord, protect me from trouble; You surround me with songs and shouts of deliverance. Selah" (Psalm 32:7 AMP).

20

Worship Breaks the Power of Demonic Bondage

Worship, as was mentioned before, is a form of warfare. But why would we need to engage in war when our goal in worship is to render adoration and praise to the almighty God? As we respond to God and give Him the glory due to His name, God responds to us. If He sees that His children are bound and in need of rescue from strongholds, iniquities, and sin, He is going to be moved with compassion and certainly respond. God is our loving Father who has already sent the precious Holy Spirit to loose the chains of darkness from us so we will be free to live the abundant life that Jesus died on the cross to give us.

Many times in a worship service, the Lord is setting the saved and unsaved free from demonic activity in their lives. Many of them aren't even aware that satan is oppressing them or hindering them from accepting Christ as Lord and Savior. If they have accepted Christ, satan may be keeping them bound in other areas of their lives. Once we have been saved, we truly have been transferred out of the kingdom of darkness into the marvelous light of God's kingdom. We have moved our residency from one kingdom to another. Now that we are in the kingdom of God, He is going to go to work on renewing our minds to think like the residents of His kingdom. His residents have the mind of Christ. He is going to change the way we dress and carry ourselves to follow suit with the citizens of His kingdom. He is going to work with us to destroy the bondages we obtained in the kingdom of darkness and He will heal the wounds we sustained there. We have to cooperate with Him to not just be saved from hell only but, also to be made "whole" here in the present. Becoming "whole" speaks to our mind and emotions, body, and spirit.

Once we are saved, our conversion doesn't stop there. There is much work to be done immediately after and for the rest of our lives! Even after conversion, we may still be struggling with habitual sin. Some of us truly want to let go of it but, we seem to succumb to it anyway. In our past, there may have been sins such as smoking, drugs, alcohol, lustful thoughts, pornography, lying, anger, pride, unforgiveness, bitterness, foul language, jealousy, envy, fornication, and other sins. Well, you might say, "If a person is struggling with any of these things then they can't possibly be saved!" If you have truly repented in your heart of your sins and you have accepted Christ as your Lord and Savior, you will notice that you hate being controlled by these sins. You will be desperate to be free from these sins and you will be truly sorrowful every time you fall back into them. You no longer accept them by choice as your way of life. You now want to obey the Lord and please Him. You want to be free from your past. If this is you then know that the Lord is willing and able to deliver you completely in every area of your life.

There are some believers who are delivered instantly from cigarette smoking and other sins against the body when they accepted Christ as their personal Savior. There are others who continue smoking after salvation and, even though they try to quit, or they may quit for a time, to their dismay, they are back at it again. They feel like a yo-yo bouncing up and down, over and around because they know these things are sins, and they don't please God.

It's possible that these individuals are struggling against more than just their physical body craving more alcohol, cigarettes, drugs, or sex. If they find it so hard to resist certain sinful temptations though they truly want to stop then there may be something else at play. They may be in bondage to that sin because they are being held captive by demonic forces. In other words, choices they made in their past may have opened a door, so to speak, giving satan and his demonic forces *the right* to influence them and hold them captive. They may not have been aware that taking their first drag from a joint or cigarette was going to addict them but, our enemy satan is always looking for an entryway or a weakness so he can prey on anyone. They may have only wanted to try alcohol because a family member or friend drank, and they were just curious. They may not have known that their family, for generations, has wrestled with what is called a familiar (family) spirit of alcoholism. That first drink opened that door of bondage over their life. They may have come under bondage because of their own foolish or rebellious choices and not because of a familiar spirit.

We all have made foolish choices and decisions in our lives – some of us more than others. Some of us have ended up addicted and in bondage and others have not. For all of us, there have been consequences because sin *always* brings consequences whether we believe it does or not. Listen, there is good news! There is an avenger – no not the Marvel Avengers – but the *"real"* avenger who has already defeated satan and his demonic forces. His name is Jesus! He is our champion. He is the first and last avenger! The BLOOD OF JESUS will always cause every demon, evil spirit, lying spirit, and strongholds to flee in Jesus' name!

> *Isaiah 53:5 states, "He was wounded for our transgressions, He was crushed for our wickedness [our sin, our injustice, our wrongdoing; the punishment [required] for our well-being fell on Him, And by His stripes (wounds) we are healed" (AMP).*

The blood that Jesus shed on the cross was and is for the healing of the nations. When you have faith in the power of the blood of Jesus then you can "plead" the blood of Jesus. That means that you remind satan that in the court of heaven your one and only defense for your past sins is the BLOOD that Jesus shed for you! Satan has no right to keep you bound because the price was already paid. The sentence we would have been given for our sins was carried out by Jesus! Hallelujah! You have the right to go free! Go ahead and plead the blood. Cover yourself in the blood of Jesus and declare that you are free! By Jesus' stripes, you were healed.

You are free to receive physical, mental, and spiritual healing; all healing. If you have an addition, believe by faith that you will not go through withdrawal symptoms in the name of Jesus! Declare now that you will no longer crave nicotine, alcohol, drugs, sleeping pills, narcotics, casual sex, pornography, adulterous affairs, homosexuality, perversion, witchcraft, gambling, lying, cheating, stealing, violent anger, or any other bondage. You are free by the blood of Jesus. That blood refers to the stripes Jesus received and the abuse and torture He went through shedding His innocent blood for you and me. There is power in the BLOOD! Say that with me – there is power in the BLOOD! Hallelujah!

Cover yourself daily in the blood of Jesus. Cover your family also. This will be a continual reminder daily of who has paid the price to save you from hell; who paid the price to deliver you from your sins, bondages, and strongholds; who paid the price to keep you from future sin.

Whenever you worship, whether privately or in a church service, thank God for the blood of Jesus. Thank God, the Father, for sending His dear Son Jesus to rescue you. Thank Jesus for submitting to the Father's will and becoming the perfect sinless sacrifice. Thank the Holy Spirit for coming here to earth to execute the will of the Father and to give us the power to not only receive our freedom but, to set others free!

Confess during your time of worship that you have been set free from any bondages you are aware of. Find scriptures that relate to healing and deliverance and confess them as you worship and declare that you are free from all bondage. Be specific and name that bondage and repent of it. Below are examples of scriptures you can confess during your worship time:

> *Ephesians 1:7 states, "In Him we have redemption [that is, our deliverance and salvation] through His blood, [which paid the penalty for our sin and resulted in] the forgiveness and complete pardon of our sin, in accordance with the riches of His grace" (AMP).*

Hebrews 9:14 states, "How much more will the blood of Christ, who through the eternal [Holy] Spirit willingly offered Himself unblemished [that is, without moral or spiritual imperfection as a sacrifice] to God, cleanse your conscience from dead works and lifeless observances to serve the ever living God" (AMP).

Matthew 26:28 states, "For this is My blood of the [new and better] covenant, which [ratifies the agreement and] is being poured out for many [as a substitutionary atonement] for the forgiveness of sins" (AMP).

1 John 4:4 says, "Little children (believers, dear ones), you are of God and you belong to Him and have [already] overcome them [the agents of the antichrist]; because He who is in you is greater than He (satan) who is in the world [of sinful mankind]" (AMP).

Galatians 5:1 states, "It was for this freedom that Christ set us free [completely liberating us]; therefore keep standing firm and do not be subject again to a yoke of slavery [which you once removed]" (AMP).

James 4:7 says, "So submit to [the authority of] God. Resist the devil [stand firm against Him] and He will flee from you" (AMP).

Psalm 34:17 says, "When the righteous cry [for help], the Lord hears and rescues them from all their distress and troubles" (AMP).

The word of God has power! Speak that word, memorize the word of God. Cherish it more than you do your physical food, for it is food and nourishment for the soul.

21

Worship illuminates the Soul with the Light of the Holy Spirit and the Word of God

"Behold, you desire truth in the innermost being, and in the hidden part [of my heart] You will make me know wisdom. (Psalm 51:6 AMP).

God desires that we possess truth in our innermost being and in the hidden part of our heart which refers, not to our natural heart but, to our mind, will, and emotions. Truth needs to be revealed through the Word of God. Truth should be revealed through the Word of God and from the Holy Spirit.

We think we already know the truth because there are millions of books written on every conceivable subject known to man. We think we know the truth because a professor tells us what to believe, or a news anchor tells us what to think about world events. Truth is not limited to the understanding of mere men nor is it subject to their interpretation of facts. Truth is found in the word of God which is revealed or illuminated by the Holy Spirit.

Our creator is the originator of truth! He is the author of it! He existed before the earth and nature and mankind were ever created. He alone knows the purpose for it all, how it was formed, and how it is being sustained. Outside of the knowledge and wisdom of God, all we find are theories, hypotheses, and innuendos, and man's never-ending quest to be his own creator and master of his own fate while rejecting God. To possess the truth, you must know the God of truth, who has revealed it to the world through His son Jesus Christ. Jesus demonstrated truth while He walked on the earth. He taught truth and left us the record of His life and the prophets through the Holy Bible which is the Word of God. He returned to heaven and has sent the precious Holy Spirit to this earthly realm to guide us into all truth. The Holy Spirit wants to first reveal to us what Jesus declared about Himself – *"I am the way, the truth, and the life. No one can come to the Father except through me"* (John 14:6 (NLT). No one can receive salvation and eternal life except by choosing to receive Jesus Christ as Lord and Savior. That is the greatest truth there is!

"For God so loved the world that He gave His one and only Son, that whoever believes in Him shall not perish but have eternal life" (John 3:16 NIV).

That is the foundation on which all truth is laid – the revelation that you and I don't have to perish and die and go to hell. There is a way of escape through the shed blood of Jesus Christ on the cross. No matter what you ever achieve in your life span – whether you acquire great riches, fame, or position – if you never receive Jesus Christ as your personal Savior then you lived your entire life for short-term pleasure and not for long-term eternity. *"And how does a man benefit if He gains the whole world and loses His soul in the process?"* Mark 8:36 (TLB).

What is your soul worth? Would you sell it right now if you were guaranteed great riches? Would you sell it if you were promised stardom and notoriety? Would you sell it for the man of your dreams or the woman of your dreams? For drugs? Alcohol? To get out of prison? Maybe there's someone you want to see come to justice. Would you sell your soul for their punishment and revenge? Can you name a price for what your soul is worth? If you have heard the gospel and you have chosen to reject Christ and all things related to Christianity then you have sold your soul, my friend. I believe that God is so just and righteous that everyone ever born will get to choose who will claim their soul (heaven or hell), even if they died without hearing the gospel here on earth. I believe that somehow, in His divine wisdom, God has a plan to determine whether they will spend eternity in heaven or hell. I believe this because the scriptures say the following: 2 Peter 3:9 (KJV) says,

> "The Lord is not slack concerning His promise, as some men count slackness; but is longsuffering to us-ward, not willing that any should perish, but that all should come to repentance".

Romans 8:38-39 (KJV) states,

> "For I am convinced that neither death nor life, neither angels nor demons, neither the present nor the future, nor any powers, neither height nor depth, nor anything else in all creation, will be able to separate us from the love of God that is in Christ Jesus our Lord".

God is not willing that ANY should perish. He doesn't want anyone to die and go to hell. He wants everyone to come to repentance. In Romans 8:39 (TLB) He tells us that "…nothing will ever be able to separate us from the love of God demonstrated by our Lord Jesus Christ when He died for us. That love He speaks of drove Christ to the cross to die for you and me. It was that love that somehow pushed Him beyond the degradation, the torture, the humiliation, and the hurt from being rejected by His Father so He could lay down His life. Now you and I can take up a new life in Christ that is everlasting life. It is the life we were always meant to live. My friend, the Lord Jesus must have all your soul or none of it. He will not share you with satan and the world. You must choose who is your Lord and where you will spend eternity.

Do not be deceived into thinking that what you believe is separate from how you live. How you live is because of what you believe. You can't confess that Christ is your Savior and Lord and believe that He is the Son of God who died for your sins, and you see nothing wrong with having sex outside of marriage. Would the one who died to save you from your sins participate with you in your sin as your Lord? No, never. Would Jesus have required that we confess our sins and repent of them in order to receive salvation and then turn around and ignore our lifestyle of sin? No, never.

Please, I implore you. Don't be deceived. It is not enough to *believe* in Jesus and confess the sinner's prayer. The Bible says this – "*you say you have faith, for you believe that there is one God. Good for you! Even the demons believe this, and they tremble in terror"* (James 2:19 NLT). It is not enough to go to church, serve at church, even witness, and get souls saved if you are unrepentant in your heart.

Please understand, I am not talking about you and me living a perfect life and never committing a sin. We can have assurance in knowing that if we do sin and Jesus is our Lord if we truly have Godly sorrow and we repent of it then He forgives us. What I am talking about is the habitual sin that your conscience has made clear to you is wrong in God's sight. You know that what you are engaging in is wrong and you don't repent of it. I am talking about those of us who know and understand the gospel of Jesus Christ yet, have no fear of God's eternal judgment and the consequences of our choices. You need to stop and take a moment to ask yourself, am I really saved? Am I really born again? If your life is still the same after you confessed Jesus as Savior and Lord, maybe you never committed to the Lord to turn away from your sins. Maybe you prayed a "guilty conscience" prayer with no intention of doing whatever was necessary to turn loose the old lifestyle.

Part of repentance is to turn around and go in the opposite direction. That may not be easy to do but, it is necessary. In order to live righteously and please God, you may have to drop relationships and people from your life. You may have to physically move from where you are now. You may have to get a new occupation if the current one will keep you bound in sin. You may have to make restitution to someone you robbed or swindled. You may lose a lot of wealth if you decide to live by the standards of the Bible. You may need to seek help for drug or alcohol addiction and so on. Repentance can be something different for everyone but, it is a necessary part of truly being saved.

The fruit of your repentance can also be a process. It may take time for you to get free from that ungodly situation or habitual sin but, you can rest assured that, as long as your heart and will want to be free then the Holy Spirit will empower you to be free! The key is that you must have a willing heart and you must want Jesus and salvation more than you want the old sin life. It is your choice and I pray you will choose the love of Christ and not the love of your life apart from Christ. You don't have to figure out how you're going to clean up your life and relationships, and everything you know is not pleasing to Him. The Holy Spirit is standing by to assist if you ask Him.

Right now, all you must do is say yes to the Lord and pray the following prayer:

> *My life is now yours. Do with it whatever you please. I am sorry for my sins. I am sorry for my rebellion. I have been running from you for a long time but, now, I am running to you. Please show me what to do next. Lead me and guide me into this new life of salvation with you. Teach me how to live for you. I am ready now. I accept Jesus Christ as my Lord and Savior and I thank you for the gift of eternal life. Amen!*

Now, if you don't have a church home then, right now, ask the Holy Spirit to lead you to a spirit-filled church that teaches the Word of God. That's a church that believes in and teaches the word of God especially as it pertains to the Holy Spirit and what the Bible calls the gifts of the Holy Spirit that should operate in the local church. It is important that you fellowship with other believers and find your "spiritual" family and be planted in a local church that you attend regularly. Jesus, the head of the church, set this precedent in place that all believers should not forsake the assembling of themselves together. There is exponential power available when believers join together in worship and service to the Lord.

Start reading your Bible daily and spend time in prayer. The Holy Spirit will lead and guide you into all truth. Remember that you are loved by God the Father, Jesus the Son, and the Holy Spirit. All three and watching over the word of God to perform it in your life as you surrender to their Lordship. I leave you with these two very special blessings from the word of God: Numbers 6:24-26 (AMP) says,

> "The Lord bless you, and keep you [protect you, sustain you, and guard you]; The Lord make His face shine upon you [with favor], and be gracious to you [surrounding you

with loving kindness]; The Lord lift up His countenance (face) upon you [with divine approval], and give you peace [a tranquil heart and life]".

"Now to Him who is able to keep you from stumbling or falling into sin, and to present you unblemished [blameless and faultless] in the presence of His glory with triumphant joy and unspeakable delight, to the only God our Savior, through Jesus Christ our Lord, be glory, majesty, dominion, and power, before all time and now and forever" (Jude 24-25 AMP).

Amen and Amen!

Bibliography

1 Kenneth Hagin Ministries. *FOUNDERS MEMORIAL. Retrieved December 13, 2019, from* https://www.rhema.org/index.php?option=com_content&view=article&id=8&Itemid=137.
2 Kenneth Hagin Ministries, Inc. (1975). *WHY TONGUES?* (28th edition). Tulsa, OK: Rhema Bible Church.
3 Kenneth Hagin Ministries. *SPEAKING IN TONGUES. Retrieved December 13, 2019, from* https://www.rhema.org/index.php?option=com_content&view=article&id=1283:speaking-in-tongues233&catid=53&Itemid=145.
4 Arts and Culture Religion. *George Whitefield (1714-1770).* Retrieved on December 28, 2019, from https://www.georgiaencyclopedia.org/articles/arts-culture/george-whitefield-1714-1770.
5 Whitefield, George. *George Whitefield Sermon: "The Indwelling of the Spirit the Common Privilege of All Believers".* Retrieved on December 13, 2019, from https://www.biblebb.com/files/whitefield/GW038.htm.
6 Kenneth Hagin Ministries. *Seven Reasons Why Every Believer Should Speak in Tongues. Retrieved December 13, 2019, from* https://www.rhema.org/

index.php?option=com_content&view=article&id=1053:seven-reasons-why-every-believer-should-speak-in-tongues&catid=53&Itemid=145.

7 The Azusa Street Revival. Retrieved on December 28, 2019 from, https://www.apostolicarchives.com/articles/article/8801925/173190.htm.

8 Wellington Boone Ministries. *About Bishop Wellington Boone.* Retrieved January 9, 2020, from https://wellingtonboone.com/about

9 Boone, Wellington. *Holy Spirit Is My Friend.* Appte Publishing. 2011. http://WellingtonBoone.com. P. 170.

www.ingramcontent.com/pod-product-compliance
Lightning Source LLC
Chambersburg PA
CBHW071827080526
44589CB00012B/936